An Immigrant's Tale

India to Canada

Inasu George Nadakavukaran

An Immigrant's Tale
Copyright © 2020 by Inasu George Nadakavukaran

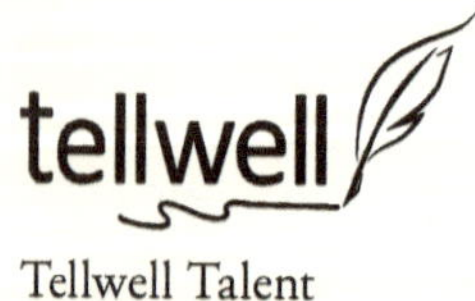

Tellwell Talent
www.tellwell.ca

ISBN
978-0-2288-3202-7 (Hardcover)
978-0-2288-3200-3 (Paperback)
978-0-2288-3201-0 (eBook)

Dedication

I want to dedicate this book to my siblings
and my passed away parents

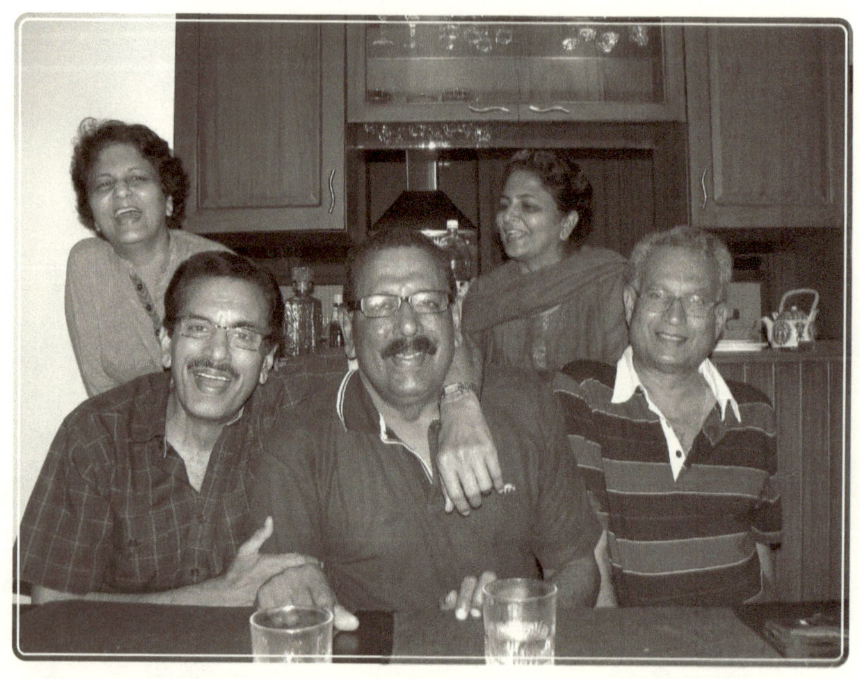

Eldest sitting on right sitting on right N.Mathew George,
sitting centre N.G.Jose. Sitting left the author

Standing behind left Hansa Johny, standing right side, Annie Cherical

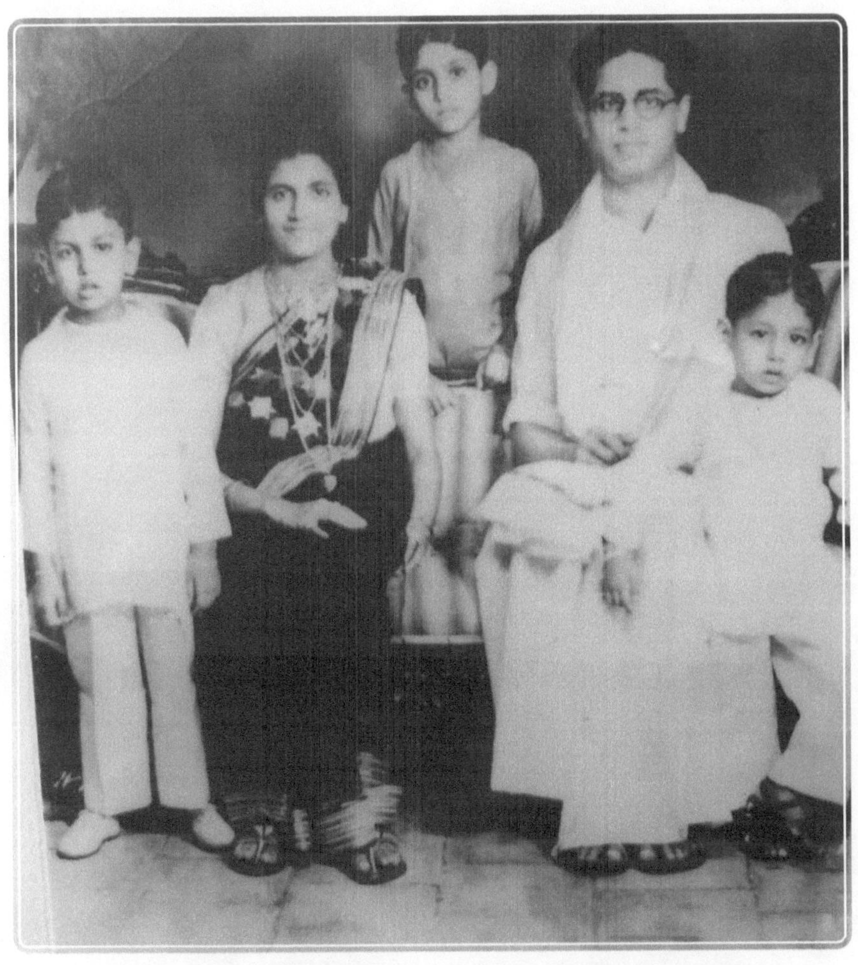

Sitting on right is dad N.I.George, sitting on left mom Elsy George

Standing on right is Jose, standing on left The
author, standing behind is Mathew

Table of Contents

An Immigrant's Tale

INDIA TO CANADA

It has often been said that you never fully appreciate what you have in your own back yard. This is so interesting, how often we ignore the wonders that are around us, while it is easily available or accessible. For example, I was born in 1944 at a place called Trichur in Kerala State in South Western India, blessed with scenic beauty, literacy and spices. Kerala State is a narrow stretch of land with Arabian sea on one side and 8,000-feet-high Western Ghats Mountains on the other side. As a result, we get lots of rain in the Monsoon season, which starts in beginning of June and lasts till end of August every year. That is also popular time for tourists, who enjoys the rain. Everything is bountiful and beautiful during the Monsoon, including water falls. Rainforests and lakes. Kerala Government is promoting Monsoon tourism in this season. In summer time, tourists come here to enjoy the beaches and some popular festivals, couple of famous festivals are Onam and Thrissur Puram. While I was in Kerala, I had taken all these for granted, but later on whenever I revisited Kerala during holidays from Canada, I realized the beauty of Kerala and wondered how I missed these enchanting attractions, while I grew up there in bygone years.

There is so much to do here, Luxurious houseboats with modern facilities are available for rent on the lakes in Kerala. There are lots of lakes, in Kerala. Some of them called backwaters. These house boats come equipped with cook and captain. The captain navigates the backwaters through lush greenery unique to this area. While cook will be preparing delicious meals, mostly Kerala style. They will also stop at market place to buy fresh fish from fisherman to cook special dish according to your taste.

Kerala is rich in beauty, culture, diversity and tolerance. It has a population that has the highest literacy rate in the world. All religions get along very well. You can see a Christian church, Hindu temple and Mosques all within few yards away from each other. Not to be forgotten is a 500-year-old Jewish Synagogue in a predominantly Muslim populated area. Keralites participate and celebrate each other's festivals.

Kerala has had a varied history which has been shaped by various foreigners. St Thomas, one of Christ's disciples came here and established Christianity almost 2000 years ago. The very first Church, Mosque and Hindu Temple in India, all were built here. Vasco da Gama, came here from Portugal for spices in 14th century. He played a major role establishing Catholic churches under Pope Martin V and converted lot of Orthodox Christians living in Kerala to Catholicism. For his contributions, in 1524 Vasco da Gamma was appointed Governor of India. That is enough about religion.

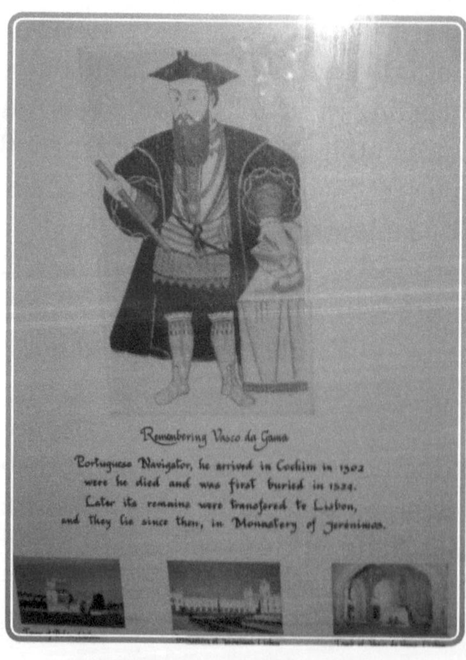

It is truly God's own country as labelled by the *National Geographic Magazine in October 1999 issue,* listed Kerala as **"One of the 10 paradises of the world"** and also included in the list of **"50 of the world's top destinations"** that every curious traveler should visit in a life time. In fact, my North American friends and acquaintances who has been to Kerala, wonder why someone like me would leave such a beautiful place to spend majority of my life in North America.

Ah, that is the story that I want to tell you about, my journey into the unknown at the young age of 25, when I thought the grass was greener on the other side of the world. Needless to say, Canada is also beautiful place, it is just different. You see, before I left India, I travelled through the Kerala state by train many times without paying much attention to the beauty all around me. This has changed and now I appreciate the land every time I visit and take the train journeys in Kerala.

By the way Kerala means land of coconuts. You see coconut trees everywhere. We use coconut trees for everything. For example, we use coconut oil for cooking, fibre for making ropes, leaves for making thatched roofs and toddy, which is very popular alcoholic drink in Kerala. I didn't pay too much attention, for all these things, while I was there. But it is not just me, I met few Canadians who lives only 100 km away from Niagara Falls, never seen falls. When I asked them, they told me oh, it is on our back yard it will be there always we can go there anytime, one of these days we will make a trip there. I thought myself, exactly my sentiment. I never seen Taj Mahal either until I lived 40 years in Canada. This is so interesting how we often do not appreciate the wonders close to us. So, open your eyes, before you move to Canada, you may not get another chance to see what you have in your country. I watch lots of travel shows on television also, travelled to 21 countries, e very country has its own beautiful places. We take it for granted when it is easily available or convenient. We only appreciate these things, when we are away or not available anymore. So, enjoy what you have, before it's lost. Look around and capture the moments and cherish what you have. World is changing, lot of things going to disappear due to climate change and developments. Lot of these problems are created by humans only, with uncontrolled developments without proper planning. So, enjoy what you have, tomorrow won't be the same. So, bring with your good old memories you cherish.

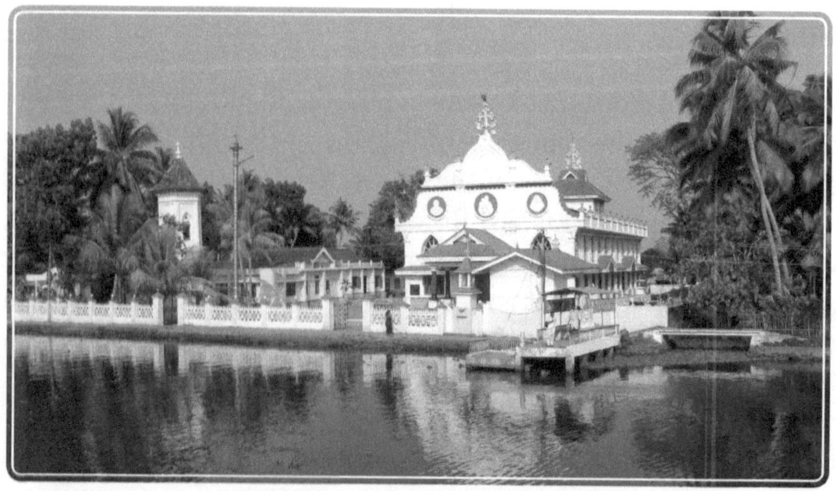

A river side church in Kerala

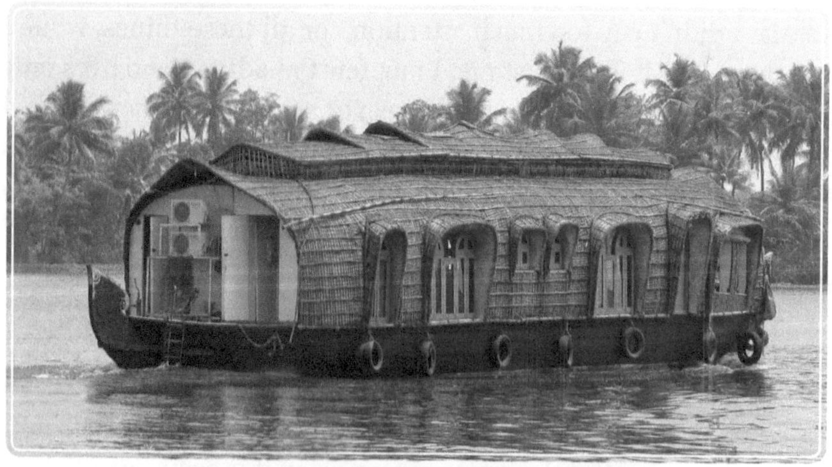

House Boat

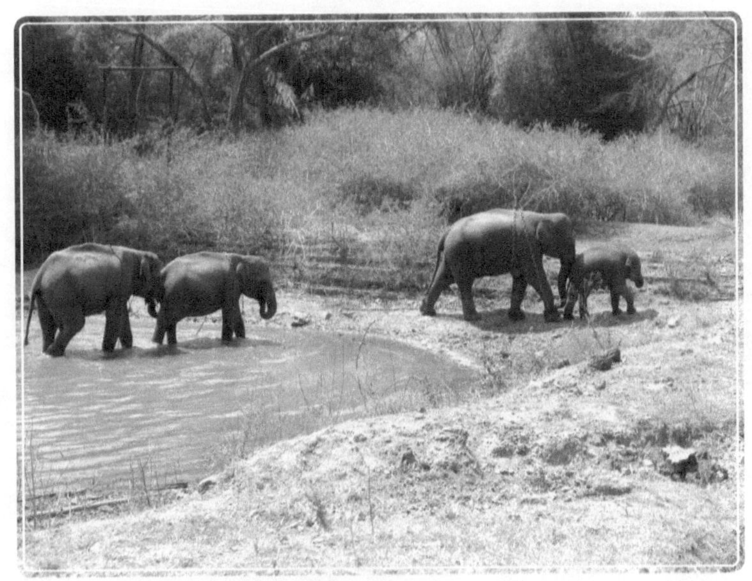

Elephants crossing, they have right of way

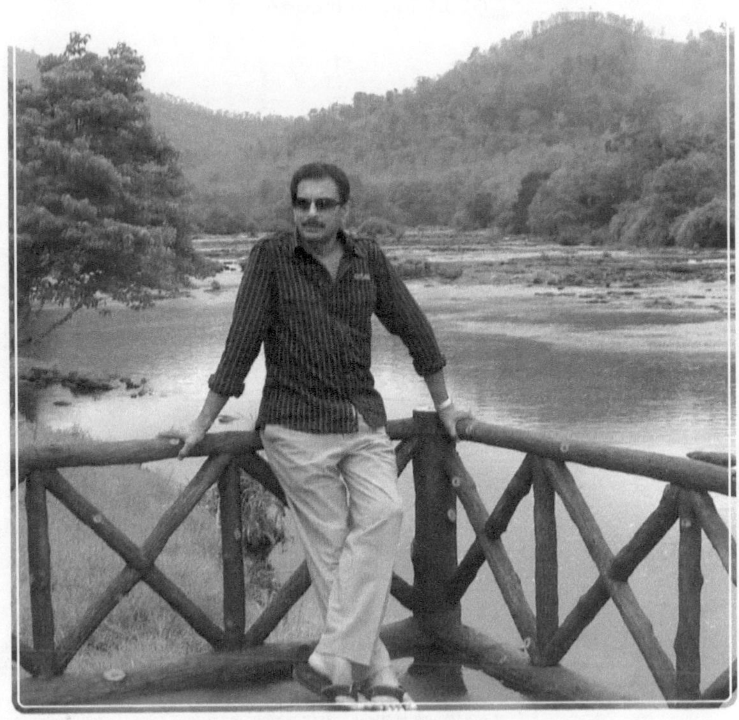

Author enjoying home land

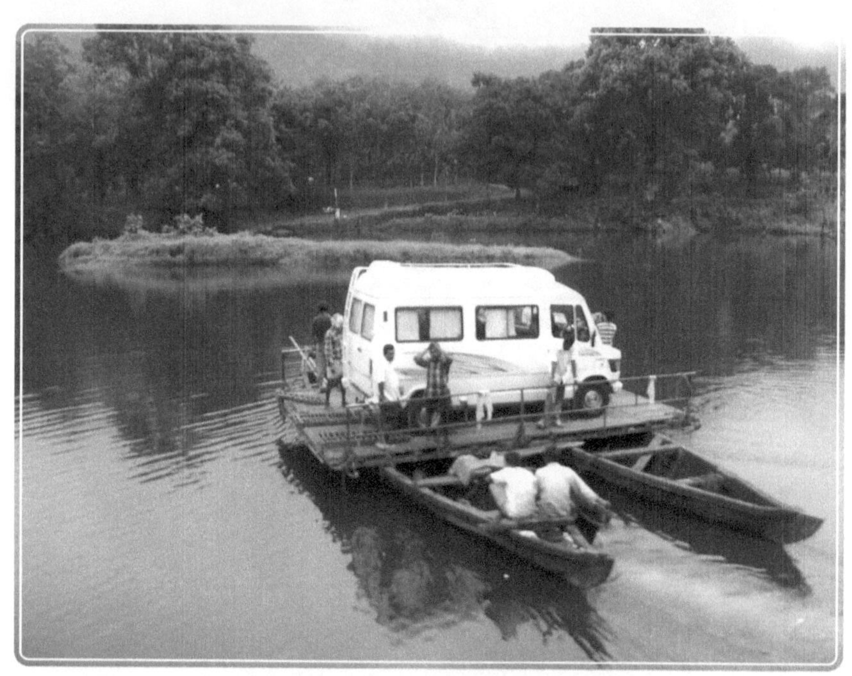

No bridge no problem

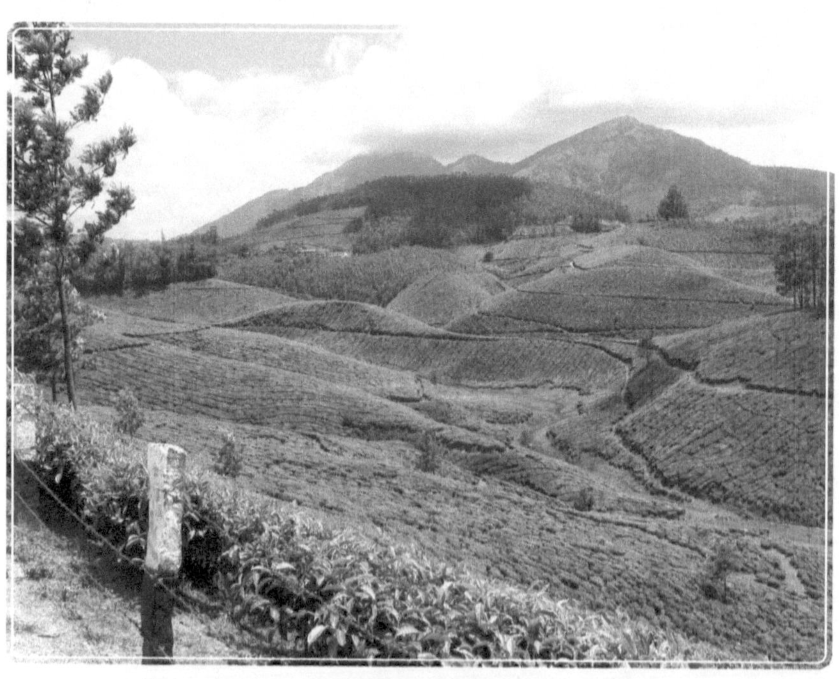

Munnar Tea Estates

Family History

My family comes from a long and storied lineage, I was born into Nadakavukaran family. Now don't try to pronounce it. During 1794, on an invitation from Sakthan Thampuran, then king of Cochin State, 52 Christian families were brought to Trichur for trade and Industrial development. One among the 52 was Nadakavukaran family, its prominent leader was Kannampuzha Nadakavukaran Ittiachan. Mr. Ittiachan and his successors known for their integrity, sincerity, uprightness and hard work. Since then earned a lot of respect in the society. The local rulers and the English were so pleased with their performance, that many of them were elevated to enviable positions. Our ancestors, left lasting impressions in the field of wood industry, agriculture and land etc. Later they diversified their activities into the field of contracting to build major structures. In appreciation of all their meritorious services, they earned a lot of laurels.

Before 1957, Kerala was divided into three states known as Travancore, Cochin and Malabar. Trichur was capital of Cochin. We were the only one capable of building certain projects in the whole State. For example, we built a dam called Peechi Dam to supply water to the city. Dam is built between two mountains to capture the water of the river. Dam looks so solid to last 1000 years. I remember visiting this dam during its construction with my father when I was very young boy. I still remember its enormity of the structure. Those days there were no heavy equipment, most of the work were done by manpower. We also built auditoriums, office buildings, highways and even outside the state, buildings for Madras Christian college. Even after more than 100 years later, these are all still famous structures. Unfortunately, The Great Depression did not spare us and during that time, we lost lot of business. Most of our properties were sold to pay off the liabilities.

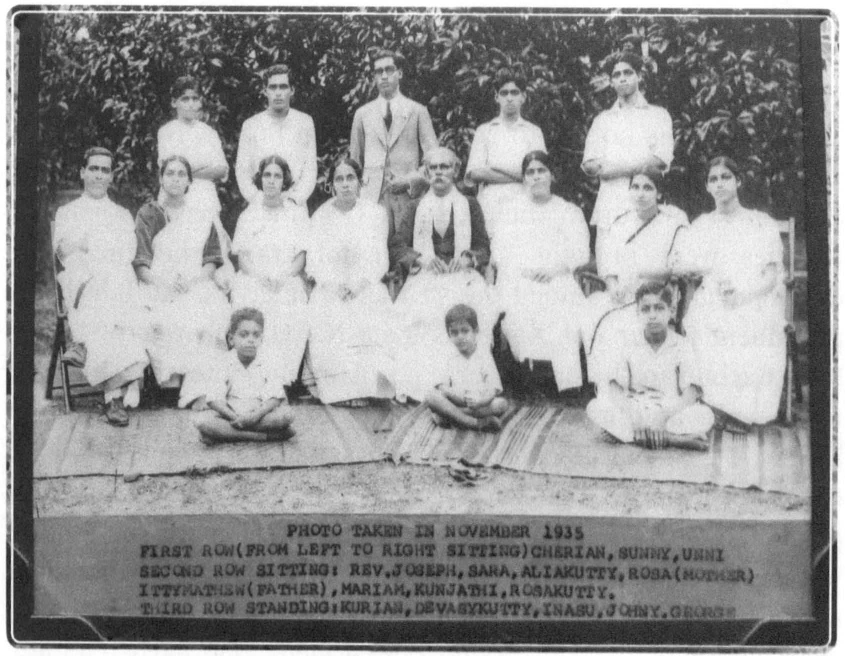

Dad's parents and 14 siblings

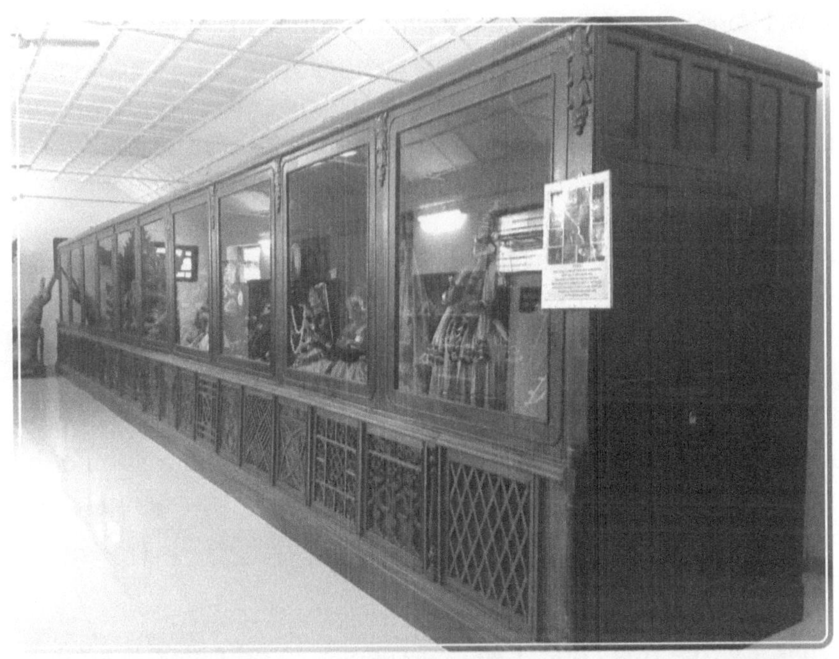

Grand father's donation to museum. It is 50 feet long cabinet for exabits

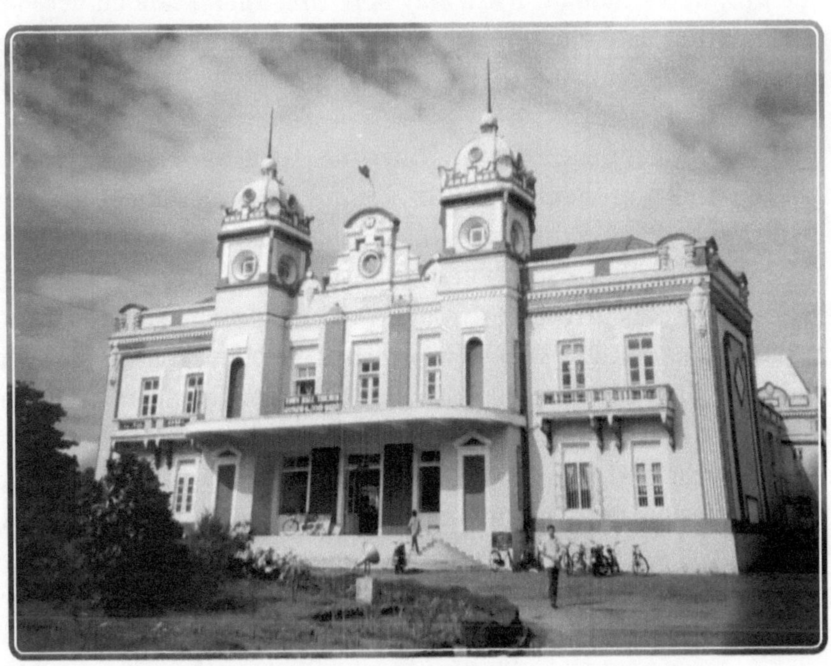

One of the ancestors built who also built Peechi Dam,
built this auditorium called as Town Hall

Now, I hope you are sitting down while reading this. It may shock you to know that my dad had 14 siblings, they were 9 boys and 5 girls, all from one mother. So, I have cousins all over the world. Now, my uncles and aunties all passed away. I have fond memories of them. Generally, they were all jolly good fellows.

My mom is from Ollukaran family, and they were 7 siblings, they were 3 boys and 4 girls. So total, I had 19 uncles and aunties. More the merrier. My mom's parents were into business. They owned whole sale business, gas station, also they owned cashew estate. My grandfather donated 50 acres of his estate to church to build a seminary for priests. He also allowed to built a church on of his property. For his contributions, Patriarch who is head of our church presented him a special award and gave him a title called "Athleta" which means church champion.

When I wrote this book, I was 75 years old and I have lived more than 50 years in Canada, that is half a century, where did all the time ago, never thought I will stay here that long. I landed here as an immigrant, in June 1969. It took more than one year to complete immigration process in India.

Many events happened during this time. I got married, have two children and 6 grandchildren. It is quite an achievement and all seemed to happen seamlessly while blending my childhood culture and values with that of a nation so far away from home. For instance, my marriage was arranged through the indulgence and support of my parents using age old custom which they followed for their own marriage. This custom allows the parties to be comfortable with each others history and social background. Proposal usually comes through extended families or friends. When you think about it, matrimonial sites and dating services perform similar activities and can be considered a form of arranged marriage. My wife is coming from another town about 100KM away. My aunts' husband was her mom's cousin. This is how this proposal came. Now you get the general idea, how this works. Divorce is also getting very common in

India. Now a days, living together before marriage is also common especially in big cities. 50 years ago, when I left, it was not that common. So, now there is not much difference between two cultures. India is changing rapidly, some times more rapidly than you want. I hope they will retain some of the rich cultures. Scientists from IIT Kharagpur and Archaeological Survey of India have uncovered evidence that the Indus Valley Civilization is at least 8,000 old. I am sure we can learn lot of good things from that civilization.

I did not ask my children to follow the old custom, they found their own life partners. We met the girl's parents before wedding, just to plan the wedding and to introduce ourselves.

My eldest son's wife's parents are originally from India, but settled in Canada. We met them at a restaurant at Brighton, Ontario. Her father is a retired professor at Saskatchewan university and mother is a retired teacher. They have settled down at Ottawa after retirement.

My second son's wife's parents are living in India. They flew from India to meet us, at Rochester New York where my son is doing residency program. Her father is a Wing Commander in Indian air force and mother is a retired teacher. They are living in Delhi, India.

My parents also, were married at Trichur, mom was only 14 and my dad was 24 years old. Those days, people married at very young age. Now it is generally frowned upon and sometimes illegal to marry that young. Now most often young people want to experience life before making a commitment to marry. My parent's marriage in 1940 was a grand affair as captured in the photo of their wedding procession which shows numerous cars, that were not that common to see on the roads. The wedding was so spectacular it was documented in the local and state media. It is now been immortalized and a search of Trichur in Wikipedia shows photo of this wedding procession.

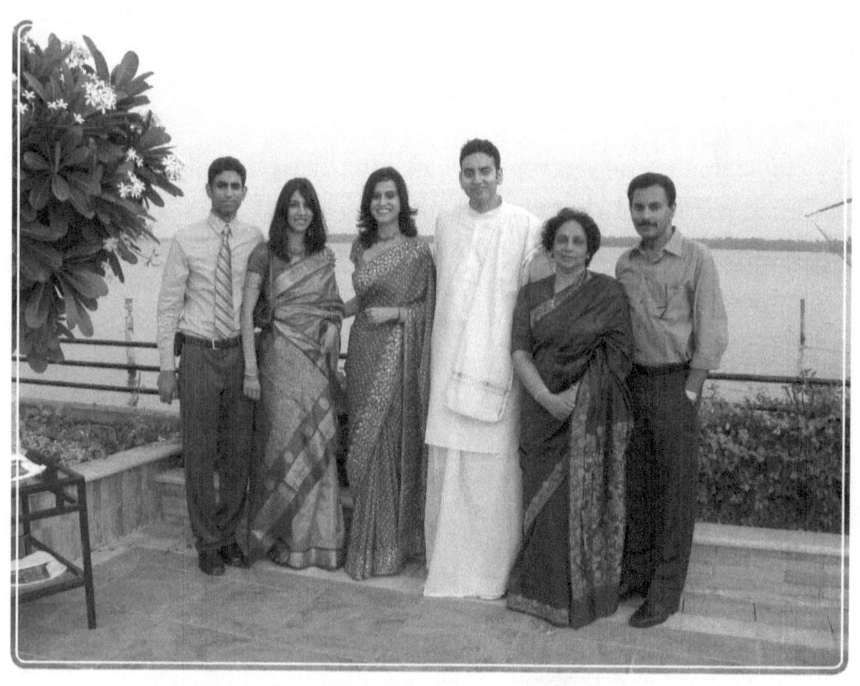

Two sons with their wives, with author and wife

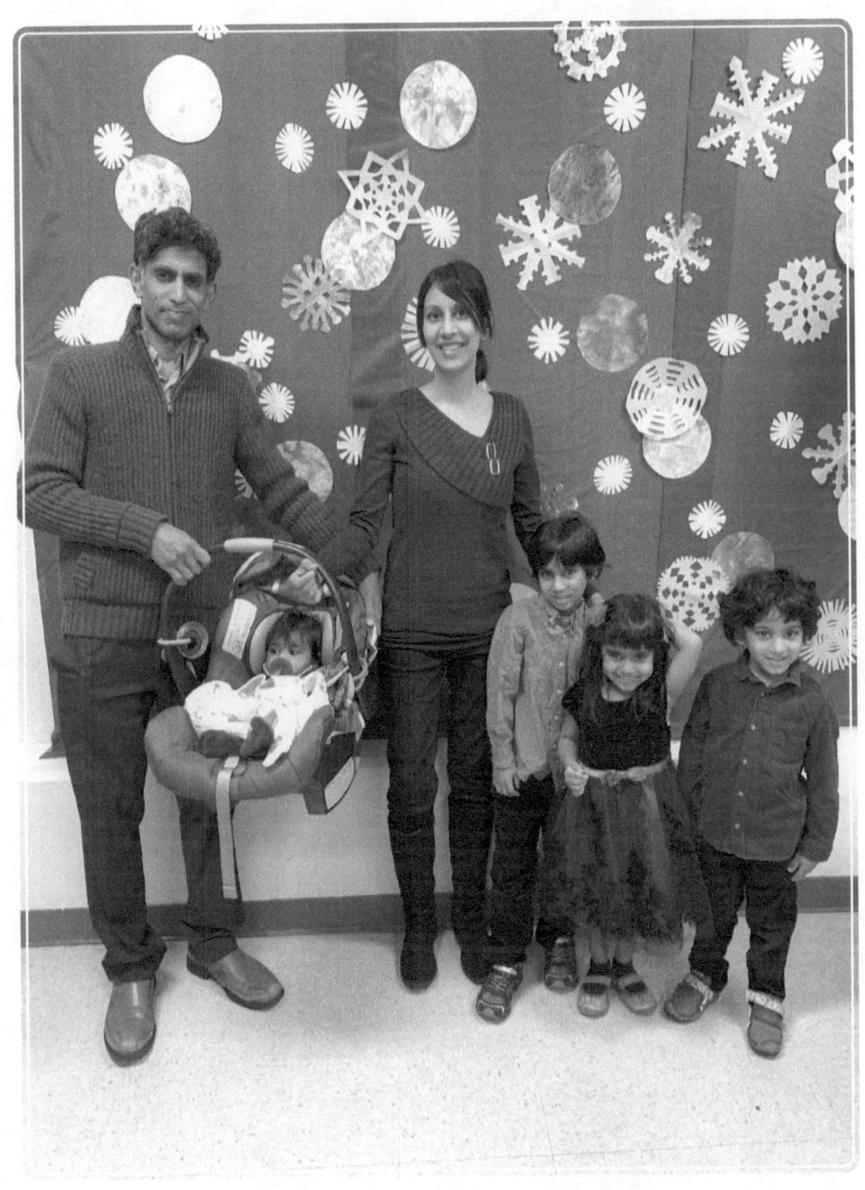

Eldest son and wife with their 4 children

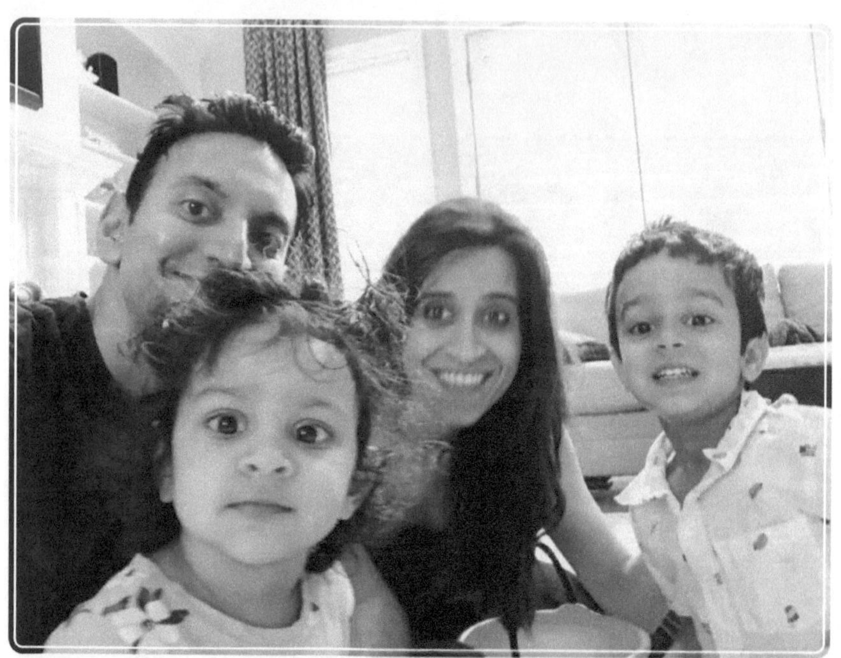

Younger son and wife with two children

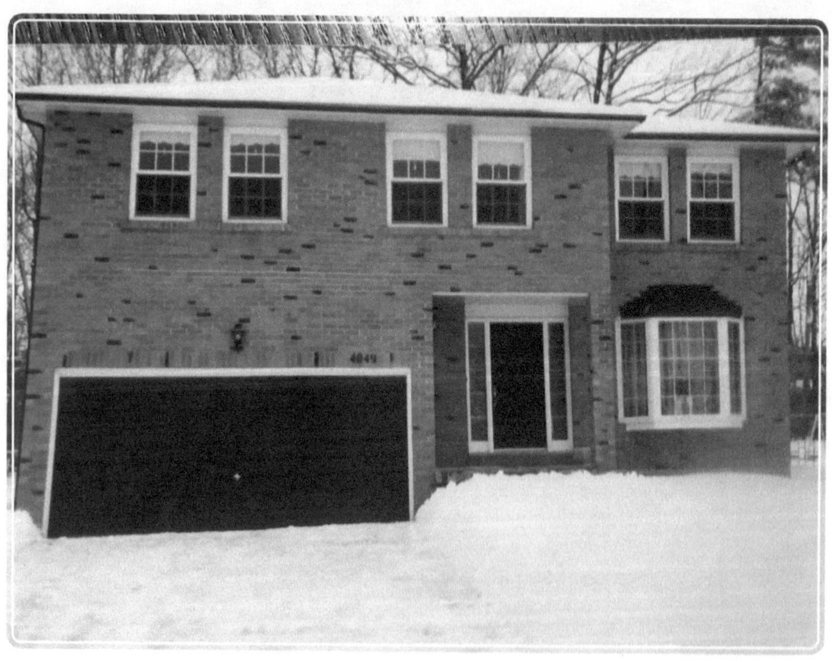

House children grew up in Canada

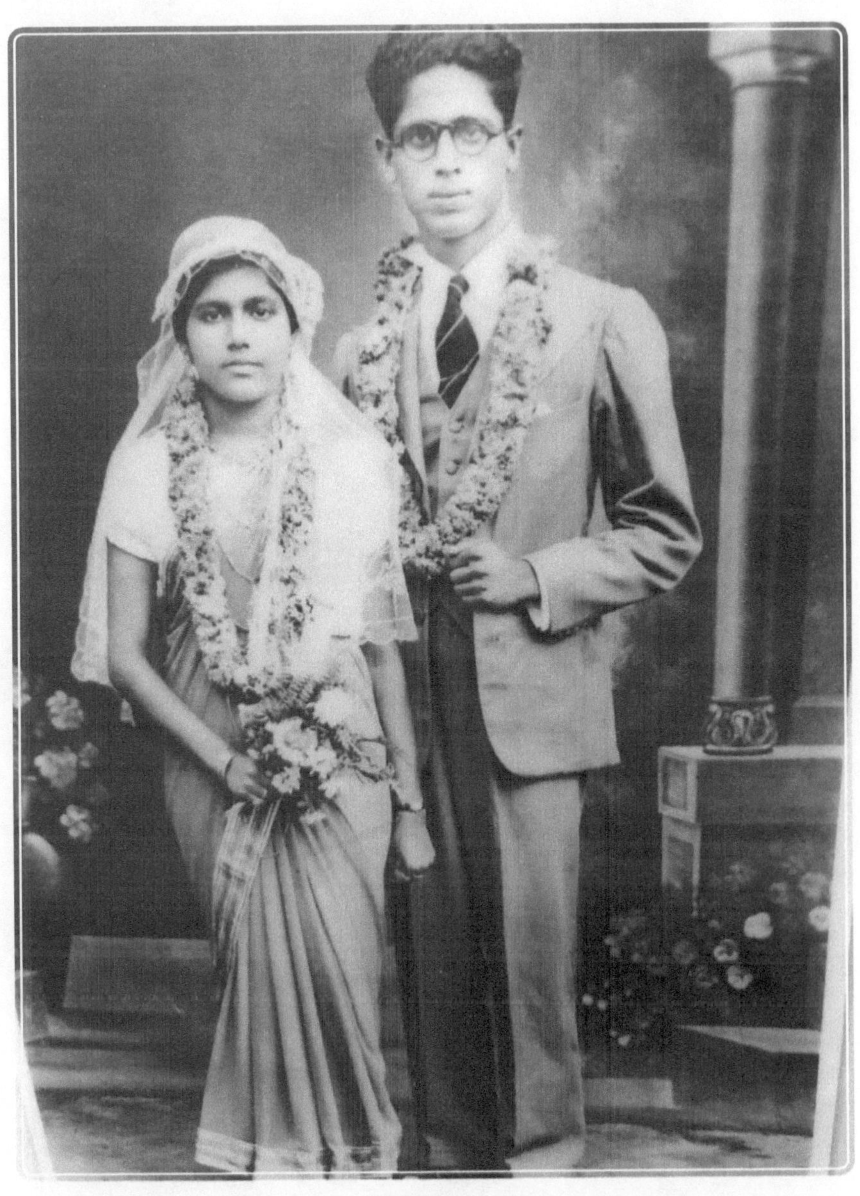

Mom and Dad's wedding photo in 1940

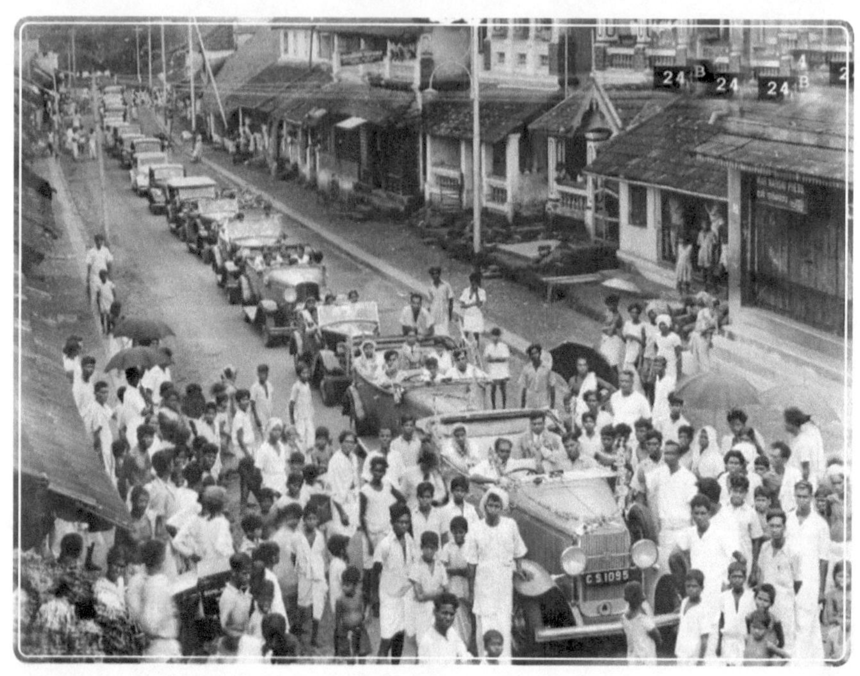

Wedding procession

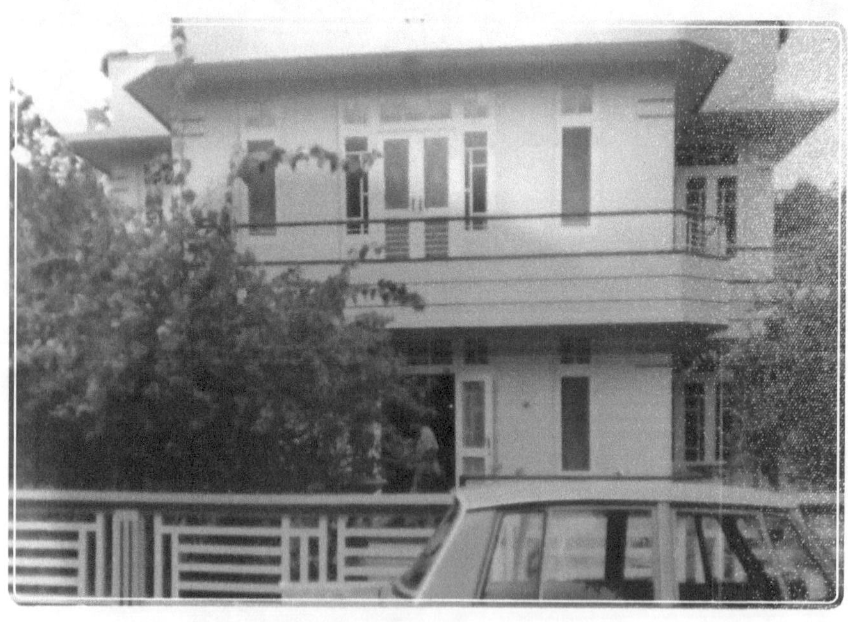

House where I was born and also where mom lived until marriage

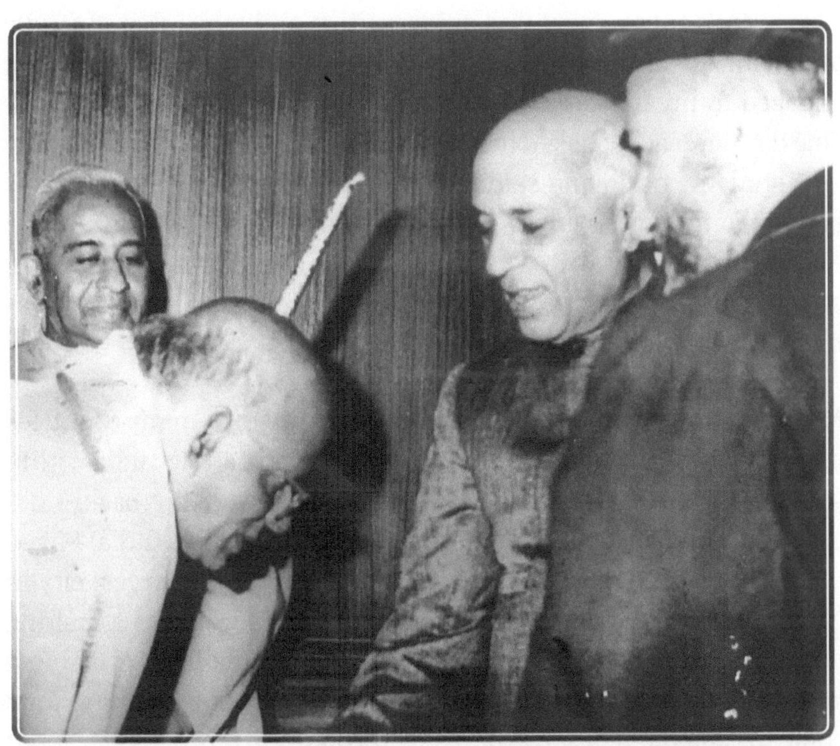

Grandfather meeting Nehru, then prime minister of India.

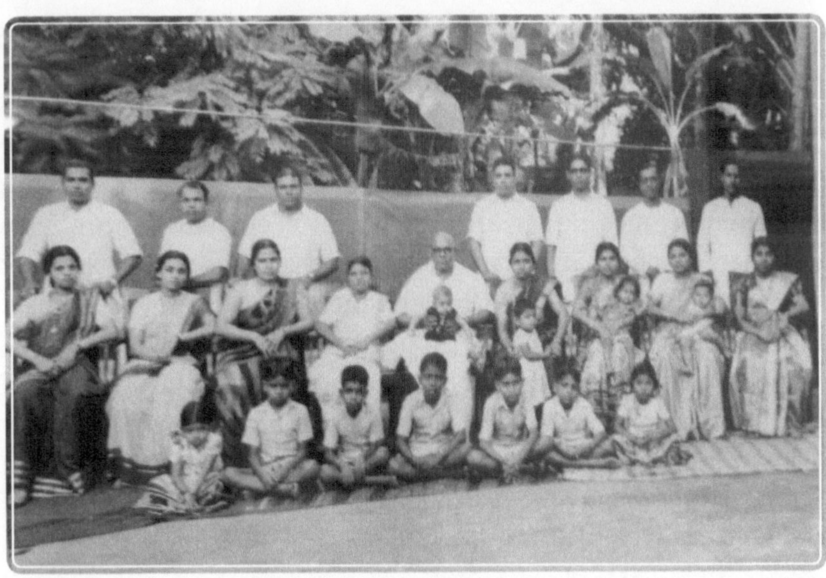

My mom's parents, siblings and their children. Author front row, second from left

My parent's engagement was quite exciting and remembered fondly and with lot of amusement. My dad was a teacher when he got engaged to my mother and who was a student in the same school. One day her teacher asked her class name an animal with big cheeks. One student got up and said my mom's name. The whole class was laughing and jumping with this funny joke. This teacher went and told this to my dad who was teaching another class nearby, he had so much fun hearing this. And he never hesitated to repeat it to us many times, when we were young.

My plan was to immigrate to Canada and travel to as many countries as possible and see all different cultures, and go back to India within 3 years of time. I am still here after 50 years. Looking back; I did the right thing to stay here. All my adult life since I left India, I lived in Toronto only. Toronto changed a lot, it became 4th largest city in North America, ranking include Mexico City. Toronto is a melting pot of the world; majority people are immigrants here. It is most culturally divorced place in the world. Still half of the immigrants come to Canada, will settle down in Toronto, currently that is about 150,000 immigrants every year. So, this is one of the reasons Toronto real estate is very expensive. Now a days, lot of immigrants come here with lot of money, especially from UAE, Hong Kong, China Russia and some other countries. They can afford to buy houses here.

I will write more about Toronto developments in later pages. So much has happened during this time, lot of people are no more with us. Technology moving at warp speed and still doubling every 5 years or sooner. I wonder if we can live without all these gadgets or ask ourselves how did we live without all these, but life was lot simpler. You don't have to remember all these pass words or carry a cell phone wherever you go. Now can you live without Google or other social medias. How much information is available on your finger tips? Now we are talking about Artificial Intelligence, 5G technology, Bit coin and Block Chain. Lot of people may not have heard about of some of these, but soon it will be a household name. Remember what famous scientist Steven Hawkins warning about Artificial Intelligence, it can take over us and control us. Whether it will happen or not, it is a scary thought. Below I will write my life as an immigrant and my first 25 years life in India. Most of us here are immigrants and everyone of them will have a story to tell, I hope you will enjoy reading this book. I also liked to hear other immigrants' stories.

Growing Up in India

As explained earlier, I was born in a small town Trichur in Kerala state, in South India. In Kerala, we speak Malayalam. It is one of the Indian languages. In India, everyone should learn three languages, one is English, then Hindi and in my case Malayalam. Hindi is the major Indian language. All Bollywood movies are made in Hindi. Did you know India is the largest English-speaking country in the world? This was huge advantage to India over other countries in IT field. You will see young Indian IT professionals all over the world. In India, every state has its own language, on top of that each language has its own alphabets. Then there are more than 200 dialects. So, anybody speaks English, he can converse almost anywhere in India. All road signs and legal documents are in English and one of the Indian languages. It is a miracle; India still is a democratic country and staying together as one nation. In Canada, we have only two languages, and we still have problems keeping country together. I really hope it will remain as one country. I can't imagine, why a country such as Canada supposed to be the best country in the world want to break up. Hope and pray, it will never happen. Queen Elizabeth is still honourable head of the government and our Governor General is her representative. Prime Minister is elected leader of the majority and forms the government. Parliament MPs are all elected, but senate is appointed. And we call ourselves a democratic country. It is too complicated for me to understand. In my opinion, there should be political will across the nation to make changes on the constitution for the sake of longevity of Canada. In my opinion Senate should be abolished or elect the members there. Well, I said my piece of politics. I have lot to say about politics, but this is not the place to express my ideas.

I was second among five siblings. My dad was a bank Manager, then chief Auditor and when he retired, he was in charge of all personnel in State bank of Mysore. After retiring, a private bank offered him job as General Manager, but he worked only one year there due to health problems. My mother was a housewife. I have one older brother and one younger brother and two younger sisters. Youngest sister is the brainy one, she was a teacher, she still does consultancy work for other schools' Other sister was more interested in social activities and volunteer work. Sometimes her photo and write up comes in the newspapers. I always joke with her, by asking how much you paid news paper to put your photo in the paper. Younger brother was in Pharmaceutical business, then he was teaching other company representatives in India and abroad. My eldest brother followed Father's foot steps in the bank. He wants to join in armed forces, but my dad was not very happy about it. Finally, he decided to take dad's advice, and all his life he complained about it, even though he was the most hard-working staff in the bank. Growing up was lot of fun, my dad being sportsman, encouraged us to get into sports. He created a sports club at home. So, all our friends come to our house to play soccer, badminton and other sports activities. We were living in a large property, we also had swimming pool. So, it was lot of fun. He was very strict also. After 6:30PM you should be at your desk studying. Otherwise you will see another side of my dad. I mean you get beating with a cane. I never seen this as a problem, It is all part of growing up in those days.

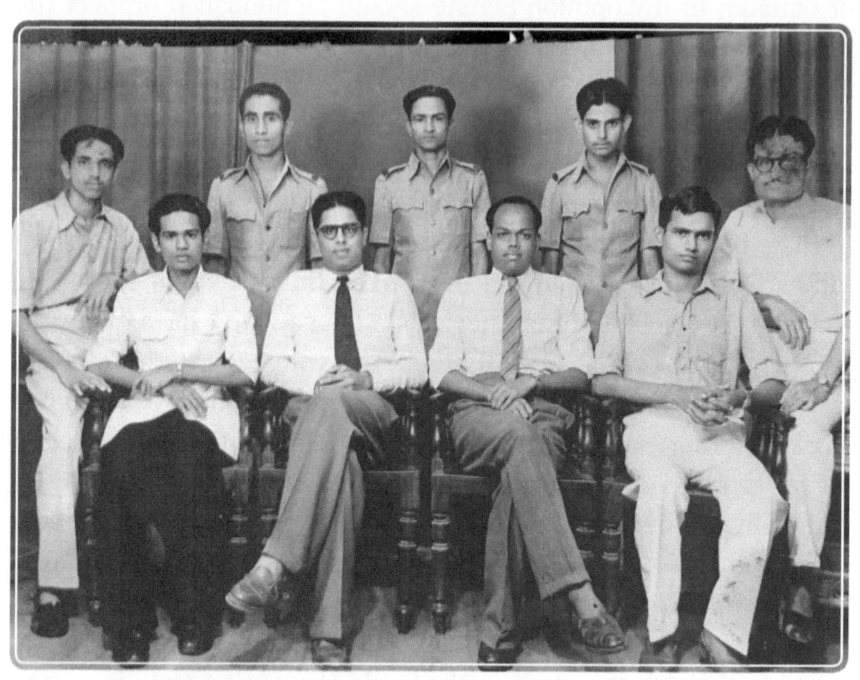

When he was bank manager, dark tie and glasses

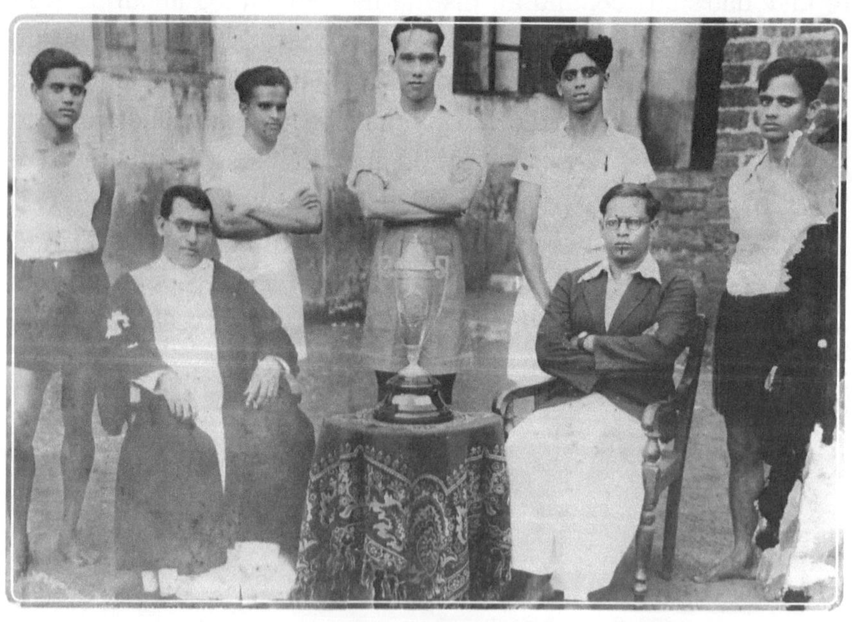

Dad with track and field, standing back row, right side

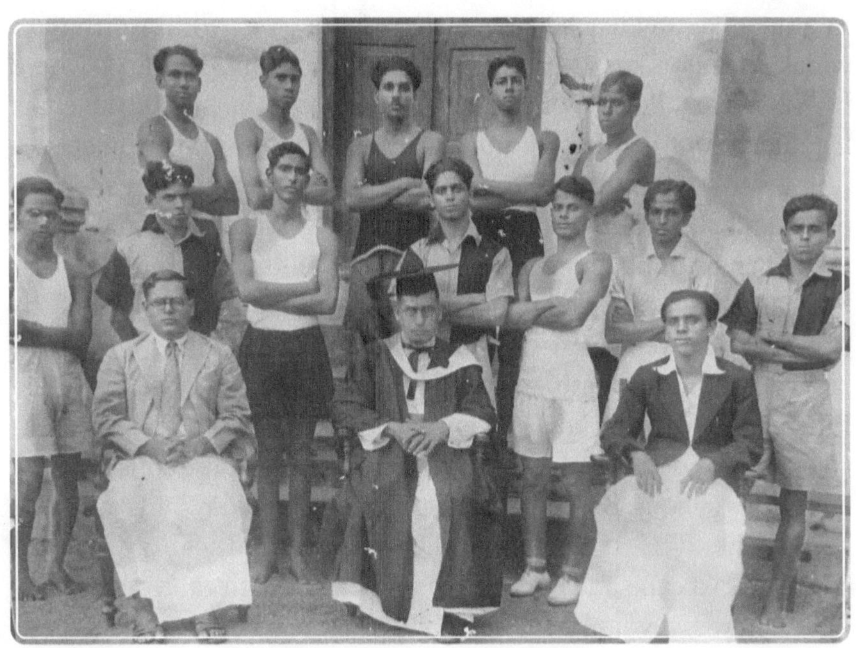

Dad when he was college captain, standing second row middle

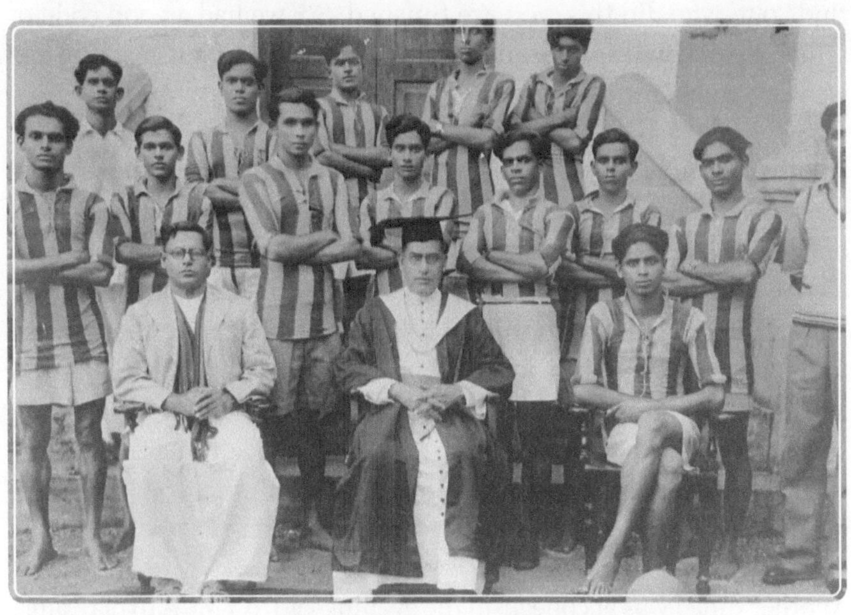

Dad soccer team captain, sitting right with soccer ball

I will give you few examples of the punishments in those days. I was in grade five, my teacher was a short fellow, we call him "Thund", which means a small piece. Our school roof used to leak where he sits. Instead of moving his chair and desk, he sits in the chair leg folded and holding an umbrella in the class. Have you seen a funnier scene than this? So, I laughed in the class, so he called me down and started to beat me with a cane and told me stand up on the bench as punishment. I was standing on the bench adjacent to the wall. So, I wrote down his nick name on the wall in Malayalam "Thund". Can you blame me for that? So, he called me down and gave me few more beatings on my calf and there were visible marks. When you wearing shorts, it is very hard to hide the marks from your parents or anybody else. On every Saturday our mom gives oil bath to everybody. So, she was putting oil on my body and saw these marks. She didn't tell me anything, but went and told my dad. He comes with a cane and I got few more beating with cane on the calf. I guess it was my fault. So, in the class, we used to cut with a razor blade half way at the joints of the cane. Every time teacher uses the cane on somebody, pieces fly off the cane one piece at a time. If he finds out, who did this, you are finished. So, we had a good code of ethics, no one will snitch, and inform the teacher. Even at young age we were good at it.

Another example, I was afraid of water, so learning swimming to me was out of question, my younger brother all learned swimming. My dad had enough of this, so he stood in middle of swimming pool with a cane and asked me to jump and swim to him. I had experienced taste of that cane many times, so I thought better die than swim. Can you imagine, I just jumped and swam to him. That is how I learned swimming and he was very happy. I didn't know learning swimming with a cane was that easy. My advice to parents, don't even think about that method to teach swimming to your children, you may end up in jail.

Another time I was at college, in the evening I go to YMCA to play table tennis, I love this game, didn't know the time, so I asked my friend what time it is. He said it 7:00PM. I told him; you mean 6:00PM. He corrected me no 7:00 PM, I dropped the bat and ran home, you must have guessed why? Because 6:30PM rule still applies whether you are in college or a young boy. I don't want to tell what happened next. Now a days your parents or teacher cannot touch you. Before his career in the bank he was teacher and scout Master. So, he taught us lot of things, even scout songs. All of us still remember those songs. He was a leader in the church and involved with youth groups, actually he was very popular in church and outside social activities and banking circle. He has won gold medals for honesty and hard work, while working for the bank. He was very influential person; we were all proud to be his children. In India, we use long last name for official functions only. His official name is N.I. George. Stands for Nadakavukaran Itty Mathew George. For many people N.I. George means Never Idle George. They use his initials to call him that way.

Other thing I was feared most was snakes. The town we lived was famous for venomous snakes. I was scared of them. Actually, at the local zoo, they had the greatest number of venomous snakes in the world. One day, I was doing my home work at night in my room, I got up walked to a cabinet to get a book near the window. Suddenly I saw a small snake coming towards my feet from under the bed. I saw it is coming towards me, I could have run, but my feet froze, couldn't move. It came and touched or licked side of my feet and returned to where it came from. Then only I was able to run and calling out for dad. When I told them, they thought I was dreaming, because this was inside the house. I insisted and told them what I saw, finally we found the snake under the bed and killed it. I still don't know why it didn't bite me only licked me. May be snake thought I am his mother.

With dad's transfer to another bank our family shifted to Cochin, now it is called Kochi. This was during Communist Rule in Kerala. All students went on strike to bring the Government down. I don't remember what was the reason. All the schools and college were shut down. Finally, President took over Government and Communist Government dismissed. There were lot of violence. I remember myself and my cousin was chased down with knife wielding communist rowdy paid by the Government. We ran and escaped to our church. When the rowdy tried to follow us into church, our priest blocked him, so he turned back. This was during the transition to Kochi. By the time we tried to get admission in good schools, there were no seats available. So, I end up in worst school you can imagine. I have seen things unimaginable to me. Teachers won't get into the class; they were scared of boys. Out of 66 students only 6 passed. I failed and lost one year.

My mom was an excellent cook. Her 7 course dinner parties are very popular. She also makes wine from almost anything. When guests come to our house, she is ready with different sorts of wine to serve them. She makes wine from grapes, Nutmeg fruit, ginger, rice, wheat and other things. Now in India you have to be careful when you visit somebody's house. They always offer you dinner or lunch or snacks depends on the time. Once they start to feed you, you have to be careful, because they don't know the meaning of "no". They just feed you weather you want it or not. One time my cousin and his American wife came for dinner. So, my mom was serving her 7-course dinner. She was serving first item, and American lady really liked it, so mom was continually feeding the first item. My cousin's wife didn't know there were 6 more items to follow and she was full already. But she didn't have a choice, she ends up eating everything. My cousin's wife still talks about it, she adores mom's cooking

My mom was also an avid Gardner. She got the first prize for the best garden in the city. It is so funny, that she did not even enter in the garden show. What happened, Judges were inspecting the gardens which was entered in the garden show, while they were walking on our street, they saw the garden and asked mom, why are you not entering the competition. They said this is the best garden they have seen so far, they forced her to enter the competition and she won the price. You will see a photo in this book, where mom standing with the award.

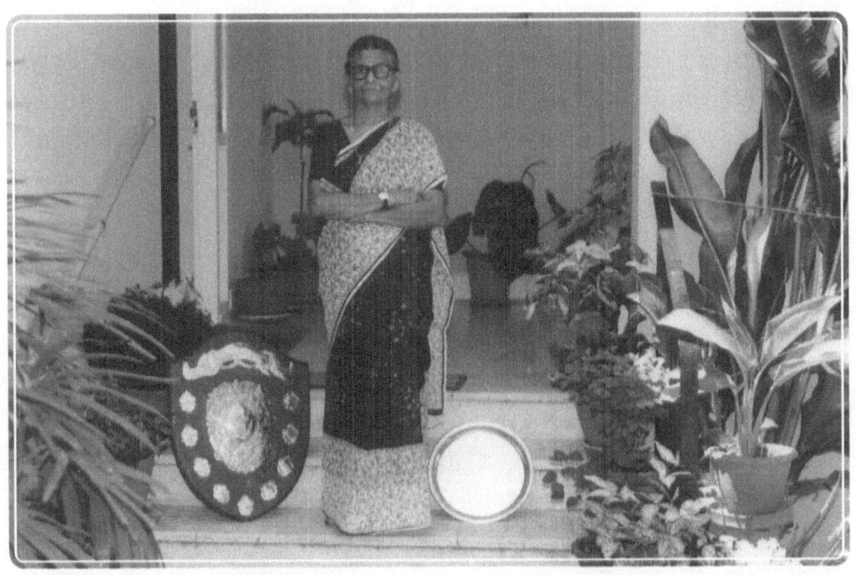

Mom with garden show first prize award

After my dad passed away, she lived alone in this house. She kept busy herself looking after her garden. I will tell you know what happened one day. Somebody knocked at the door, she opened the door. It was a robber with a knife in the hand and demanded money and gold. Robber pushed her down and she fell down, it was funny robber placed a pillow under her head to make her comfortable. She called out some people's name, pretending they were working in the back of the house and that she is not alone, hopping it will scare the robber and he will run away. He didn't fall for that, so she told him go ahead and you can stab her, but I don't keep any money or gold in the house. Robber got confused didn't know what to do and he ran away. He was a young robber and must have learned she is living alone and figured it may be too easy to rob her. Same time he was a compassionate robber, who will place a pillow under your victim. He must have thought, this is really a crazy woman. Mom must have realized he won't actually stab her. Have you heard anything like this, that is our mom? She had such a sense of humor until, she passed away. She was bed ridden for few years, but never lost her sense of humor, she used to joke with everybody. She loved to entertain the guests. Once I won the fancy-dress competition, she made me dress like a merchant lady selling snacks on the street. She also plays, pranks with neighbours. We had continuous flow of visitors at our house, and they were always welcome. Generally, people on Western countries won't understand this. Here we make an appointment to visit somebody or wait for their invitation. I don't think anything wrong with this system. I believe, in olden days there were no phones at many people's homes, so they just walk in, if you are not home, they just go back. I guess now a days, people call before they visit somebody, because everybody has phones. Even now I don't think, they wait for invitation, they just call to make sure if somebody is home and inform them, if you are home, we are coming there. In other words, they invite themselves. I don't think that is going to change for long time.

One thing I admire my parents, we travelled many places as a family. This, I still have in me, I loved to travel. Our Grandfather had a vacation home in blue Mountains in Coonoor, Tamil Nadu. So, all my school summer holidays we spent up in the Mountains. Let me tell you how I broke my elbow here. Myself and my cousin was hanging from garage door frame, it was a rectangle bar, so, very difficult to hang on and his older brother pushing me to swing and my older brother was pushing my cousin to see who can swing farther. I couldn't hold anymore, so I shouted to stop. But he doesn't want to stop and he wants me to win, I fell down broke my elbow. So, what happened, instead of helping me they all ran away afraid of punishment. Finally, our neighbour lady found me sitting in the corner of garage supporting broken hand with other hand. She went inside our house and told my grandmother. They took me to the hospital, and all my left hand was covered with plaster after two months it was removed and everything went well. My poor cousins all got usual punishment.

It was a beautiful hill station, with lots of tea estates and gardens. Climate was very pleasant in summer time. You are about 8,000 ft high and British had built beautiful roads going up there. You have to go through many hairpin bends to reach there. I still remember in the centre line they had installed bulbs with heavy glass on top to protect it. This will help you to see the road in heavy fog. I never seen this anywhere in the world. It was hard to maintain so; we don't have it anymore. You can also go up there by train. Train has to go through many tunnels to get up there. You see beautiful scenery on the way, also lots of monkeys. Middle of the two-railway track, there is rack to connect the train to climb the steep mountain. This is the only rack railway in India. UNESCO has recognized as one of the historical railways. This special railway was built by British in 1908. All the houses had beautiful gardens. Sometimes you really get very thick fog here, then a wind comes opens up the view. I never forgot those panoramic views. Lot of British decided to stay back here after India's independence. For British it was like their home. There is lot of English medium private schools and private clubs. Ever since staying in Coonoor, I loved mountains, when I see a mountain here in North America and if there is road going up to the top. I will drive up there. Here I enjoy driving through Rockies, Blue ridges mountains and Smokey mountains. Last yar I did 26,000 KM road trip and, in that trip, I climbed many mountains, even some mountain passes, I crossed were more than 12,500ft above sea level. They were all snow covered and I had choice go through less treacherous routes, but I choose mountain route. It was spectacular.

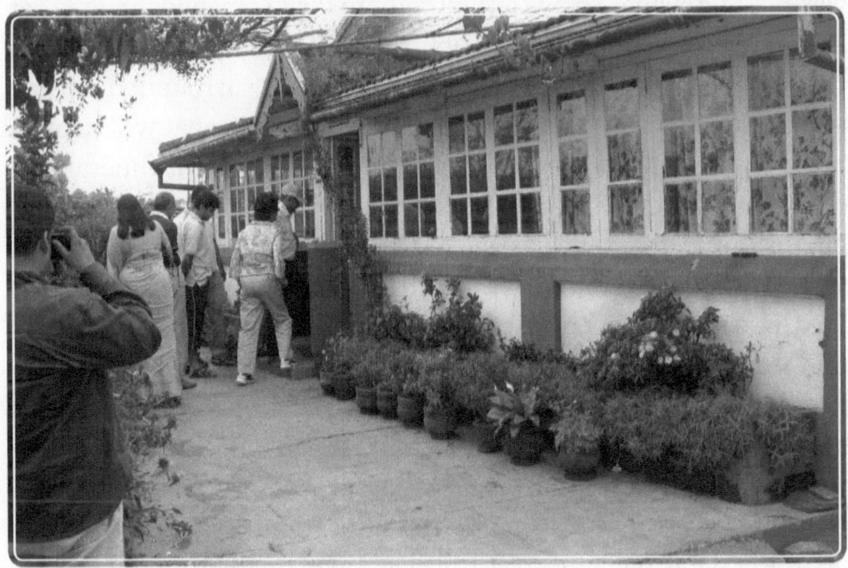

Summer cottage in Coonoor

Politics in India

One thing I don't like the politics in India. People get involved in everything; in a way it is true democracy. But I don't think, you will see many things what is happening here in other democratic countries. For instance, they call it Harthal, usually called out by opposition party. When they call out tomorrow is a Harthal day, everything shuts down. You are not allowed to drive cars and all transits will be shutdown. All the shops will be closed. If anybody dare to challenge, they will throw stones and causes so much havoc. I personally got into trouble one time during my visits there. I didn't know a Harthal was declared in certain part of the State, it was not Statewide. So, we left our city to visit somebody in another city. I was travelling with my siblings, not aware of the Harthal on the way. So, suddenly a group of motorcyclists surrounded our car and threatened us. I was really scared wondering what will happen next. So, we made an excuse that we are attending a funeral and didn't know about Harthal. They said it is in the paper and was not buying our excuse. Luckily one of the guys, may be their leader, let us go with warning not to return this way, before Harthal is over. For these reasons, you won't find many industries in Kerala. Kerala's main income comes from tourism and foreign remittances from Keralites living abroad. Actually 25% of GDP of Kerala is from this source. In comparison to rest of India, it gets only 3%. Despite all these, generally Kerala considered as prosperous state. They are well known for its health care and education. Rest of India look up at Kerala as one of the best places. I personally think, it is little bit over rated. But I see lot of potential there. Lot of credit goes to current communist government, for, health care and education. I must admire how they handled current COVID-19 crisis. I don't think, any where else in the world, can come close to Kerala how they handled it. Actually, one should learn from them so, all nations will be ready to handle the crisis.

Another time I was travelling in a bus, I saw group of people standing on the road we are travelling, when we reached there, they were signalling to stop. The driver sensed danger and tried to get through the crowd without stopping. So, the crowd started to throw stones and whatever they can get. I ducked, but some people got injured in our bus. Driver thinks, if he had stopped, anything could have happened and didn't want to take that chance. We later found out there was an accident earlier which involve a bus. So, they were taking their revenge on all the buses coming through that road. India is very difficult country to rule. Despite all these progress in India, there lot of things has to be changed. In India we have very highly educated people and the same time lot of ignorant people. One day, I was looking at a photograph in the paper, showing group of people with sledge hammer destroying solar panel farms. They believed solar farms will destroy the energy of the sun. Another politician speaking to crowd in a village, mostly farmers saying if you take electricity from hydro electrical power, then the water coming out is not good for anything. Now please don't laugh, it is true. While I was writing this book, I just heard in North America, some people were destroying 5G towers, because they thought, this was the reason, we have COVID-19 virus problem. It just shows there are ignorant people everywhere.

I personally think it will take two more generations, before we can see major improvements, in the attitude of the people in India. There are so many other things I don't approve what is happening there politically. Politicians have too much power. There are young people with excellent qualification coming and want to clean up all these things, but politicians, some of them ill qualified, has more authority over them. Politicians are the new kings in India. One hope I have for India, 50% of population is below 25 years old and more than 65% below 35. It is expected in 2020 the average age of an Indian will be 29 years, compared to 37 for China and 48 for Japan. This is a huge advantage for India. I hope this well-educated young generation is going to make huge difference in India and India will become one of the leading economies of the world. I only hope young educated people will get involved in politics and get rid of these corrupt generation from the government.

Life at Swiss Institute in Kerala

In 1962 my dad got promotion to go to the head office and all the family shifted to Bangalore, except myself. I went to study in a Swiss Institute in Northern Kerala. It was my first freedom from home, staying in hostel there. Ah: freedom how sweet it tastes; it was lot of fun; our institute was on top of a hill with a river flowing around and close by there is a nice beach. Almost like a private beach to us. It was very pretty area. Swiss staff at institute was excellent teachers. All the latest equipment came from Switzerland and Germany. We got along very well, they participated in all the sports with us. Can you imagine, we didn't have to pay anything, I mean no tuition fees, no room rent and food was also free. To get admission, you have to pass practical and theoretical exam followed by an interview. They select only few people. So, the pocket money we get from home, is just to spend on movies and once in a while to eat in restaurants. Even when we go on college trips to other cities, we don't have to pay anything. I never forgot those 4 years, of course we got in trouble also some times not obeying the rules. Myself and Two of my best friends, who lives in Australia now got in trouble disobeying a strict order not stay late at very popular temple festival. We three went and came very late. Next day, as expected we got suspended for two weeks. So, I took off to Bangalore to spend time with my family, I was worried, that my dad may get mad with me, that didn't happen. I guess he is mellowed little bit. So, I had good time in Bangalore and when I went back, everything was normal, but I had to catch up in studies with rest of the class mates.

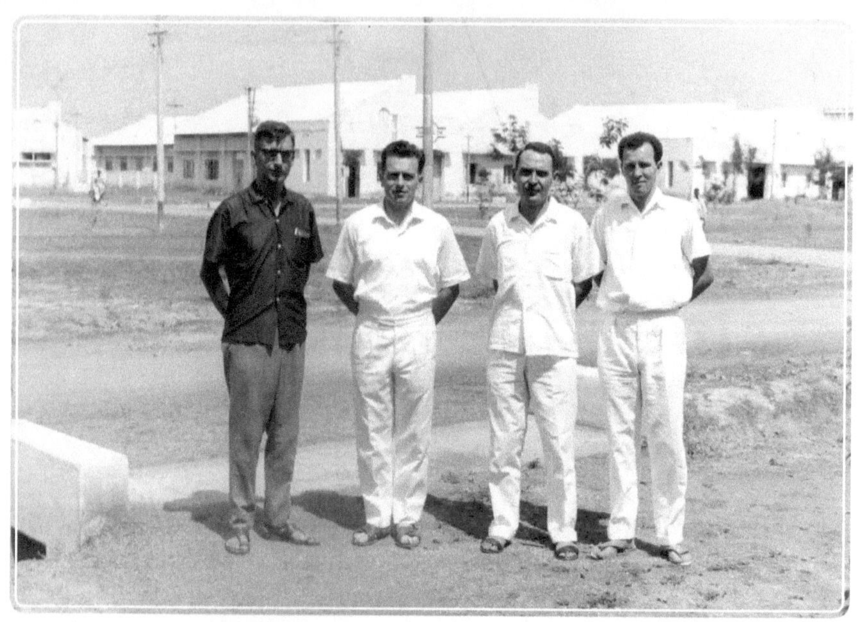

Swiss staff

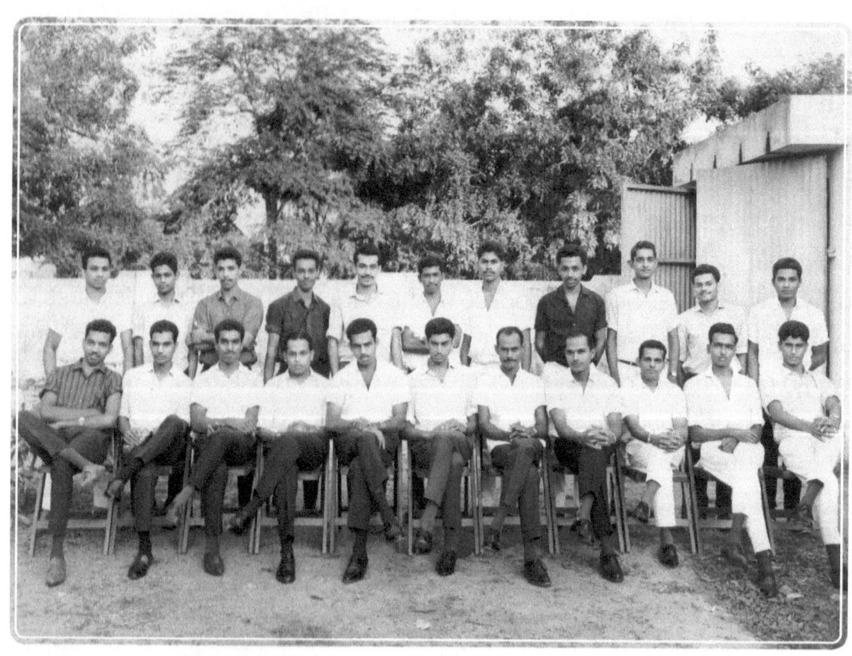

When I left Katpadi to take up a job in Bangalore
Sent off party to author sitting in middle

I really enjoyed going to movies with my friends. I never seen so many movies in my life, every week we see three movies, two Hollywood and one Bollywood. This was norm. At home if I can see one movie in a year, I would be lucky. Another time we went to Bangalore, part of a study tour. Last day of the tour, we went to bed at 11:00PM my friend told me, we came to Bangalore and we didn't even have beer. Bangalore was a beautiful city with lots of pubs. We both never had beer before, so we jumped through the window with out waking up our warden. We were at the pub and ordered two beers. I had my first sip and said Chee this is beer, it tastes terrible. I thought it will taste sweet. So, my friend gulped both glasses. Then we came to pay the bill, there was rowdy looking like Yule Brynner, the Hollywood actor grabbing people standing near the counter and punching them and the guys were rolling down to the street. I don't know what was wrong with that guy. We didn't want to take any chances. We just ran away without paying the bill. That is my first experience with alcohol. North Kerala was dry area, that means no alcohol. Anywhere there is prohibition, there is thriving black market. So, we enjoy occasional drinks at these places.

One of the best things I enjoyed here was western music. We had a group of students came from a nearby city called Mangalore. They were excellent musicians. I mean the best, as a matter of fact in all India competition in Bangalore we won the first place. It is not spelling mistake; Mangalore and Bangalore are two different places. I will never forget moon light boating with these group. Some times we were invited in nearby college to perform. We also conducted a very large concert to collect the money for Indian defence, during the war with China. It was very successful concert; all the city was talking about it. Even our Swiss staff was amazed. We also wrote a signed letter to Indira Gandhi, then prime minister of India, volunteering our services to join the army. She wrote us back thanking us stating, that India will benefit more from the training we are getting from Swiss Institute and asked us continue to complete the training and help India.

Training here was one of the best you can get from anywhere in the world. We had latest equipment and measuring instruments. All was made in Switzerland and Germany. No Japanese stuff, those days nothing can beat Swiss German quality. We had one to one student and teacher ratio. The report card goes to home every month. You have to study; they don't believe in last minute studying. Indians have bad habit, study till last minute before exam. The night before our exam, we went to far away empty building and close all windows and preparing for exam, suddenly our Swiss Principal coming through an open window and got mad. He told us if you had studied every day, you didn't have to do this. He ordered us all go to a movie. Can you imagine our nervousness when we entered exam hall? He was right, we all passed the exam. I respect my Principal so much, he was so straight forward, also don't buy silly excuses. One example, we used to go and buy rice from Mahi in black market. Mahi was a French Colony, so they have different rules. We always have freedom to use college jeep. So, this time Principal stopped us and asked where are you going? So, we told him, we are going to buy rice from Mahi. He stopped us and told I will let you use the Jeep, but not to buy things in black market and this is why India is in this state. If you don't get rice eat something else. So, he ordered us eat wheat that day onwards. Actually, I loved this wheat chapati every day, but lot of students had hard time adjusting to it. After the successful completion of the 4-year course, few of us was selected to work in their company in Katpadi, Tamil Nadu. One thing is for sure, jobs are guaranteed for students coming out of this institute in good companies, either in India or aboard. Representatives from Australia, Malaysia and Singapore will grab the students as soon you complete the course. Few of us came to Canada with out any difficulty. Some of them started their own companies.

I didn't like the Life in Katpadi and couldn't tolerate living there. it was very hot place to begin with, temperature hits 45 degree Celsius, and nothing much happening there. Only one good thing was, my best friend was also selected to work there, so I had good company. Basically, Katpadi was a boring place for me. So, I always look for any excuse to go to Bangalore by train where my family lived. Brindavan Express train will directly take you to Bangalore from Katpadi. So, it was very convenient for me to go home. I remember, one-time Katpadi was hit by very powerful cyclone, glasses are flying down from factory roof, So the Swiss Plant Manager urged us to get out of the plant, outside was pouring heavy rains and windy. Nobody was willing to move out the plant, but was waiting on bicycle to get some relief from the storm. So, the Swiss works manager asked me Inasu you go first, I started pedal and everybody followed, but after few feet we couldn't continue, we got down from bicycles and start pushing, it took us long time to reach home to safety. I remember a huge cargo ship was broken in half and rested on the beach at Madras; I don't know if it is still there. It was a huge ship. I still can't believe how a ship can break in half. That strong was the wind. Anyway, I was still trying to get out of Katpadi. The company was sending senior students to Switzerland for experience. First, they send four of them. I didn't want to wait that long, so I got an address from one of the swiss machine and applied directly for a job in Switzerland. To my surprise this company immediately offered me job with airfare and allowances. The management didn't like the idea. They put stop to it by using their influence on the company. So, I decided to leave Katpadi and got a job in Bangalore.

I was still looking for ways to get out of India and applied for immigration to Canada. Canadian immigration called me for interview in Madras, now it is called Chennai. Interview was very successful. Those days Canada needs people with our qualifications.

He asked me where you want to settle down in Canada. I told him Vancouver, because I thought that was warmest place in Canada. He advised me I will find more opportunities in Toronto, and told me few degrees of temperature does not make big difference, He said all the houses has central heating and cars and buses all heated, so I decided to go to Toronto. Meanwhile looking for better opportunities in Bangalore. I got a very senior position in Jindal, which is very large corporation. They have plants all over India. It was my responsibility to build the plant and hiring employees and all. At young age of 25 it was amazing position. Job comes with quarters to live and a vehicle. Only stipulation was that I should sign a contract that I will stay with them minimum 5 years. When I refused owner invited me to his palatial home to convince me. At the same time, I got my immigration approval from Canada. I was half mind to sign the contract and take up the position, because I loved Bangalore. It was not the same Bangalore you see now. It was like European city, with lots of lakes and pleasant climate. Even the night life was great there, with choice of all the clubs and restaurants, we used to visit, it was a great city. Now it is all changed. Developments took over and it is now, very congested and polluted place. My elder brother told me you are young and have an opportunity to go to Canada. He advised, me not to sign the contract and go to Canada, see the world, then you come back. So that was it. Also, four friends who went to Switzerland three of them married Swiss girls and settled down there. One of them was decided to immigrate to Canada. He was also very close friend, he encouraged me to immigrate to Canada. So here my Journey begins as an immigrant.

Travel to Canada

Everybody was advising me, that Canada gets very cold so, be prepared. First, I went and bought custom made three woolen suites, and start buying things to take it with me to Canada. My uncle had studied in Wycliffe College, part of Toronto University for priest hood back in 1950. He gave me some valuable advice. Also gave me Four letters to give to his old friends in Canada as an introduction. So, I was all set to go and decided to fly from Bangalore to Toronto by Lufthansa air lines. Those days flying was very expensive. My three cousins went to States before me sailed to States, it was lot cheaper. One advantage by flying, you are allowed to stop over anywhere on the airlines route. Airlines will pay for hotel, your meals and ground transportation. I am being adventurous mind decided to take full advantage of this. So, I planned to stop over in Delhi, Athens, Zurich and Cologne. On the day of my departure, a large group of my relatives and friends came to send me off, some of them came from Trichur, which is 500km away. That is Indian way. I said good bye to everyone. My journey started from Bangalore, now it is called Bengaluru. I flew from Bangalore to Delhi. When I got out of the plane to the ground, it was so hot, it was like furnace, I thought this hot air is coming from the engine. Then I realized it is Delhi summer. Actually, my travel agent had warned me about the climate in Delhi and advised me, you have to drink lot of water. I didn't take him seriously. I thought, I am an Indian and Delhi is in India so, what is the big deal. I was totally wrong. A prearranged taxi picked me from airport to take me to Claridge's hotel to spend a night there. I thought I will never reach the hotel in one piece. Driver was over speeding and even didn't stop in the Red lights. I mean Red lights, that mean he did not stop any of the red lights. I repeatedly asked him to slow down and watch the lights. There was no change in his actions. Apparently, most of the people drive like that there. Every month about 200 people get killed in traffic accidents. Delhi is one the worst places for driving. Now I have driven in Fourteen countries, never seen anything like that. Finally, I reached hotel in one piece, thank God for that. I had good dinner; Lufthansa taken care of everything. I wish we get service like that now. I decided to write a post card to my parents about my safe arrival, anybody remember post cards, how time has changed. Now nobody writes anything, everything by email or texting or other social media. I stepped outside through the sliding door of the hotel to mail my post card, immediately stepped back, it was that hot outside, so I gave to the door man to mail it for me. I didn't mention about the taxi ride to my parents, it will give them ulcers.

Now think about it. You are travelling with no cell phone no credit cards all you have is Eight dollar in your pocket. That is how much foreign exchange Indian Government allows you to take out of country in those days. You are taking chances staying over at these places on route, even though Lufthansa pays everything., if something unexpected happens you are out of luck. I will tell you, what happened to me in Cologne later. Left Delhi, first stop was Karachi Pakistan. We didn't have to get out of the plane, it was a short stop, still I was not very comfortable there, India fought few wars with Pakistan. I thought they will come inside the plane ask for the passport and will question me. Nothing of that sort happened. But still, I was glad to leave Pakistan and we landed in Athens. It was in the morning, then an announcement came through loud speaker, calling my name and asked me to go to this restaurant for breakfast. Wow I thought what a service!!! I had excellent breakfast, then there was yellow orange juice in the glass, with my very first sip I fell in love with orange juice and still after 50 years it is my favourite juice. Next stop Was Zurich, at the airport, to go outside, only you have to hand over your passport to immigration officials, and when you return, they will return it to you. You don't need a visa to enter there. I had a coke in the airport, and I thought, wow it is not same what we get in India, everything tasted better outside India. Maybe it is just my mind. I stepped outside, one of my friends from senior batch was waiting outside. By the way he is one of the senior students sent by the company from Katpadi. I didn't know how he knew, that I will be coming. So, I didn't go to hotel. I went with him, for sight seeing and went to his place. I thought what a wonderful place is Switzerland, everything runs on time. You can set your watch to exact arrival time of trains; it was so punctual. Those days Indian trains comes hours late and will be so crowded. Those things have changed in India, but we cannot still compare what I have seen in Switzerland. I have visited 21 countries; I think I will put Switzerland on top of the list. From Zurich I flew to Cologne. Lufthansa had arranged a bus take us to town. When I arrived in town, I asked an old man about the hotel St Joseph's, where I am supposed to stay. My hotel was two blocks away, He offered to accompany me to the hotel and he carried my suitcase and walked all the way to hotel. I was much younger than him, but he won't let me carry my suitcase. He didn't speak one word in English, I thanked him by action. Now here is where the trouble starts as I mentioned earlier. The hotel manager didn't speak one-word of English, he just shaking his head and refused to give me a room. I had a pass from Lufthansa with hotel name and all, he wouldn't have any of that. I have to spend a night in Cologne, and was getting little nervous. Nobody speaks English and remember, I had only Eight dollar in my pocket and I didn't carry any credit cards or cell phone. I thought myself at least it is summer, so I won't freeze to death. So, I decided to walk to a nearby hotel, there was a lady washing dishes in the front lobby, it was not a big hotel. I gave her Lufthansa pass; didn't say one word and she gave me a key to a room upstairs. She throws the pass near to window, water flashing on the card from dish washing. I went to the room, it was nice room and clean, but I started worry, how am I going to pay. After one hour I went down, I look at the window, my pass was sitting there. I asked her to give me back my pass. She gave me back without uttering one word. To this day, I don't know why she did give me the room without any deposit or asking any questions. She didn't even to write my name in register. Maybe she felt sorry for this poor immigrant, maybe she is seeing first brown man. You cannot communicate with anybody there; they all spoke only German. So, with that pass I went back to the Hotel St Joseph's. Now there were two people, including the person who refused to give me the room and another gentleman speaks fluent English. He recognized the pass in my hand even before I showed him. He got mad with guy, who refused to give me the room and apologized to me. Sir you have room in your name here, don't understand why this guy send you away. He asked me to go to restaurant and have my dinner. Told me not worry about anything, that he will settle the bill in the hotel where I took the room. At restaurant, I look at the menu, it was all in German, so I didn't bother just said beer, that was my dinner that night, even though I could have anything I wanted there. Next morning, I took my flight to Montreal, Pilot's wife was sitting next to me, so I got fantastic service. I landed in Montreal in the evening. I couldn't believe how hot it was, thought Canada will be always cold. I was so thirsty, I asked one of the Lufthansa staff on ground where is the closest water fountain, he said you are boarding in no time, you can get a drink from the plane. I said I can't wait, so I ran to fountain got in just in time. Maybe it is hard to believe, but I couldn't wait that long.

Here is my cultural shock. In Lufthansa, people were all well dressed and well behaved all the way from Delhi to Montreal. Flight from Montreal to Toronto was in CP Air. Now you don't have that airline anymore. To my shock just in front of me two drunken and sweaty guys, trying to pinch an air hostess buttock. She is slapping on their hand, they continued until take off nobody interfered. I simply couldn't believe and asked myself, is this Canada? So far in my journey even with incident in Cologne, I was not really worried or shaken. Now, I am getting closer to my final destination. Finally, I started to really worry. I thought myself, when I land at 8:30PM in Toronto it will be dark. I didn't know summer sun sets late,

8:30PM will be full daylight. Then thought came, where I supposed to go, eight dollars is not even enough for taxi fare. So finally, I landed went through immigration, got my luggage and started to walking out then one Canadian couple called out my name Inasu, I was surprised I didn't have any idea who these people are. They introduced themselves and told me his father in law is on business trip, but asked them to pick me up and take to their home. He told me, I have a room there for you and everything is arranged. His father in law is my uncle's friend when my uncle was studying here. My uncle never mentioned to me that don't worry, I am going to write to my friend to meet you at airport on your arrival. Then there is another Indian couple saying hello to me. I recognized them immediately. I have seen them in Bangalore. We know his sister very well, but again his sister never told me my brother will be there to help you. I am not finished yet. Then there is another gentleman, who is a professor in Guelph University. He also came to pick me up. I recognised him immediately. When I was Junior school., he came to our school and given a speech. So, they all came for me, this was totally unexpected and I worried for nothing. This was Thursday night. So, I look at the group, professor lives one hour away from Toronto and the Canadian couple lives in Stouffville which is also one hour away. Indian couple lives in Toronto. I thought myself I need a job, so better go with Indian couple. Next day his wife with her one-year old baby in hand came to down town to show me where is the Manpower office in downtown. Manpower official gave me some addresses to go for interview and I visited two companies, both offered me jobs to start immediately. So, Thursday evening I landed, had interview on Friday and Monday, I started to working at Square D Company, I was shocked and bit disappointed to see the equipments here. It was all old and outdated. I am used to work with latest technology. Anyway they were very happy with me. As soon I solved one of their problems, they asked me to join their design team.

Next weekend the father in law of young Canadian couple who came to airport, invited me to join them to go to their summer cottage near Peterborough. They had beautiful property on the lake. I went boat riding with them, riding their horse in the property. Joined lot of sports activities with them in high jump and other activities. I won in most of the sports with their teenage grand daughter and grandson. We had lot of fun and enjoyed their company. Then I was having breakfast next day morning, their granddaughter asked if I want to go horse back riding in the trail with them, I asked **NOW?** (what I meant was are you going now?) what they heard was a rude **"NO"**. They all were stunned with my tone and response. Including grandparents were silent. Nobody said a word. They went horse back riding, I wondered why they all gone without me. When they came back everything was normal. Later I figured out, that is what happened. Sometimes when I speak, even I don't understand myself, so I cannot blame them. Anyway, I had wonderful time with them. They were such a lovely family. First two weeks I stayed with the Indian couple; they were very nice to me. At their I met lot of their friends. When their first son was baptized, they asked me, to be their son's God Father. I hope everybody knows what kind of God Father; this is not Mafia God Father as Marlon Brando played as Mafia Boss. From there I rented a room with kitchen facilities from a Ukraine family. Rent those days were only $20 per week.

Biggest problem was cooking. I never cooked before in my life, so I struggled and I really missed my mom's cooking. I even felt home sick. I look for the weekend to see if some family friends going to invite me for dinner. Otherwise will go to Indian restaurant. There were only two Indian restaurants then, and it was very expensive. Now there may be 500 Indian restaurants, how times changed. I assume there are 500 may be more or less. One Christmas, my friend's company gave all employees a frozen big turkey. He brought it over to my place to cook in the oven. We put the complete frozen turkey without thawing or removing the plastic bag inside with the filling in the oven. After a while, we thought something is wrong. So, we pulled it out and called a friend's wife and explained what we did. She asked us you didn't even thaw it? it is too late for that turkey dinner tonight. Told us switch off the oven and come over for dinner at her place. That is how much we know about cooking. In weekends we will hope somebody will invite us. Those days, if I see any Indian on the street, I go to him and introduce myself and we exchange phone number and will plan to meet next weekend. Then we become friends. You don't see many Indians those days. So, I was looking for a place with room and board to escape from my own cooking. One day, while walking home from work, I saw sign room for rent, and a lady was sitting in the window. So, I walked in and asked about the room. She said I am also tenant, but the land lord asked her help to rent out the upstairs room. I asked her, if I rent the room can I buy food from you. She said, let me talk to the landlord and if he agrees, she will rent all upstairs and give me room and board. I thought it was great my problem was solved. I asked her, who else are living here. She said wait till dinner time then you will meet everybody. By evening one by one, eight girls showed up for dinner. They were all from Trinidad. So, I sit at the head of the table, and everybody eight them sit around the table. I didn't know what to say, but I don't remember complaining about it. So, what happened, those girls treat me like their own brother. They asked me to go with them to Trinidad for a vacation and meet their families and all. That didn't happen. Whenever they need help, they come and ask me. Some places they don't like go alone; they ask me to go with them. One of the girls try to hook me with her sister in England, thought I may be interested to marry her. I didn't show much interest. I was a good boy there, they all liked me. What do they say, whatever happened in Las Vegas stays at Las Vegas? So, I am taking fifth amendment.

One thing my mom insisted, that I should write a letter every week and she replies all the letters. If she didn't get letter from me, she will get mad with me, once in a while she expects a phone call from me. Now let me tell you, how is the long-distance phone calls are made in those days. You have to book the call with the operator. Then when she gets connected with my mom, operator will call me and connect me with my mom. If you are lucky, you may be get connected in two hours, sometime you wait much longer. Biggest problem was, you cannot go any where or you have to start this process all over again. I didn't tell how much it cost you. It was two dollars per minute.

Think about it, those days two dollar was like may be ten dollars now. For example, an hourly rate of four dollar, considered high paying job. Another example, we used to communicate through telegram in emergency or even wishing somebody on their wedding. It is cheaper than long distance call. You have one to twenty numbers. For example, "Wishing you happy wedding anniversary" number may be 9, it is just an example. You tell the telegraph operator send number 9 and give the address. So, when they receive telegram, they will get full message. Can you imagine how much things are changed? May be younger generation don't even believe me. They may think, I am coming out of stone age. When I moved to a decent high-rise apartment, I was paying only $150 rent, now for the same apartment you pay more than $2,000.

Back in Toronto, while considering job offer with design team, I got a job offer from McDonell Douglas Aircraft company who makes DC10, DC 9 all those planes, I was making good money already, but Douglas was offering 30% more money. It was too attractive. I decided to leave Square D Company. I didn't know, when I gave my resignation, the news spread through the plant. I didn't know I am that important. They tried to stop me from leaving. I left also for another reason, my cousin was coming from India with same qualifications, so Douglas is much bigger company so we can both works together there. Finally, my cousin also joined here. I didn't enjoy working in Douglas at all. It was a place for lazy people. Very first day I was doing nothing all day waiting for a job. Nobody assigned me anything. At end of the day they asked me if I want to work Four hours over time. I told him you must be kidding, I said I don't have anything to do and didn't do nothing all day. He said it does not matter, do you want to stay? There were 9000 people working in that plant. Some of them were sleeping some where and nobody will find out. I never seen so much waste and inefficiency. They could have gotten rid off 25% work force and still be overstaffed. It is mind blowing in a bad way, how they operating this company. In Toronto plant they make huge wings and ship them to California to assemble on the body. It didn't make any sense at all. Mind you if you want to make money, that was the place.

I know some people worked 18 hours a day there. That is 10 hours over regular time. So, week days with time and half, that is extra 15 hours pay and in the weekend with double time, that is 20 hours over you regular hours per day. Can you imagine that. They had unlimited over time; you can make money hand over fist. It was not the place for me. I refused all the over time, but I was coming to work every day in a latest rental car. My colleagues could not understand this. They were thinking I am new in this country, refuse all over time, still can afford to come to work in nice cars. They must have thought I am a prince or something.

Let me tell you a funny story what happened to me in this company. I had applied 3 weeks of leave of absence to go to India to get married. They called me to the human resources office, there I met three people in the room. They asked me to take a seat and we chatted little while about my job. Then they asked me why I want the leave. I said I am going to India to get married. Immediately they all jumped up and came where I was sitting and holding me back and told me, we should not let you go, we should save you from getting married. I thought it was funny, they approved my leave anyway. When I think about it what a waste, three people have nothing much to do there to approve the leave of absence, I was not even holding an important position in the company,

I never stayed one day unemployed in Canada. My ultimate aim is to get in the automotive company which pays even more. One-time Douglas Aircraft went on strike, during this time, I took taxi license and drove taxi for a week. I didn't make much money for taxi. Actually, lost money from driving taxi. I remember I picked up one lady, she didn't know the proper address, and meter was running, so I felt sorry for her and switched off meter. You don't make money that way. And when I get back, I get parking ticket on my own car. So that was end of it. I hand over the key and left. Then I took driving instructor license, it was all for experiences more than anything. So finally, an opening came at Chrysler and I joined there. I was waiting for this job opening. There was another reason, why I want to join automotive company, particularly Chrysler car company. In India my grandfather had three cars, one of them was Chrysler and this was his favourite car and I also learned driving in that car at very young age. When I came to Canada, my first car was Chevrolet Caprice classic. My grandfather was in his death bed. My mom was next to him to say final good bye. She told him about the car I bought. He asked my mom even at his last moments "Why he didn't buy Chrysler" By the time I joined Chrysler he had already passed away. I wish he was alive, when I joined Chrysler. That would have made him happiest man. When my cousin came from India, we both were at this house with girls. Then, from there we moved to high rise apartment. One of the things, we enjoyed is going to dance halls in the weekend, there were few of them, they were huge places, still usually there will be line up to get in. We also took dance lessens at Arthur Murray studio. After few months, they were trying to make you sign long contracts, so that was end of it. I love dancing, I continued taking dance lessons in other studios. I love Latin dance and music. I travelled to lot of countries, but never been to South America or Cuba. I want to see Cuba, to enjoy Latin culture. I also want go to Cuba, before they get rid of all the old American big cars. Used from 1960's when America, imposed trade ban.

I continually looked for other opportunities. One time I visited CBC studio for voice training, suddenly someone shouted, come on guys watch the TV, first man was landing on the moon. So, I was there when Lois Armstrong landed on the moon, I will never forget that day. I didn't take voice lessons; I wish I would have done that. Now even after 50 years I talk funny, even I don't understand what I am talking about. Then I tried my hands-on real estate career. Those days it was so easy to get license. Didn't continue. I took taxi license and driving instructors license, all these I was doing, just be active. I just want to try everything. Never spent any time watching TV. As a matter of fact, I didn't even buy a TV until much later. I used to go to downtown almost everyday after work, just to walk around.

Career at Chrysler

Finally, I joined the Chrysler in Dec 1972 with even higher salary. One of the things I wanted to do was cutting short my last name, which is Nadakavukaran. Lot of people had hard time pronouncing it. People at Chrysler used to call me George Long name, George ABC, George Alphabet and so on. Some times, in a meeting people from outside ask me how do you pronounce your last name? I just say, I am not sure myself, that always brought laughter in the room. It was a good icebreaker. When I suggested to company secretary, she warned me don't you dare, she said people will remember you with this name. I am glad I didn't change my name. Now because of that long name everybody remembers me. Even an Italian company visited me and when they visited another company in Mexico. The people asked them in Mexico. Do you know George Nadakavukaran in Toronto, they replied how can we forget that name? I even escaped a police speeding ticket. It was my first speeding ticket in Canada. He was such a gentleman very polite. I never seen such decent police. He asked me to see my license and he took it from me and looking at it started to smile. I know he was trying to pronounce my name correctly So, I asked him what is so funny, he said your name, I cannot pronounce it. So, I suggested why don't you let me go, so you don't have to write it either. So, he said okay I will let you go with a warning, just be careful.

While talking about police, do you know, nobody wore seat belts, there were no shoulder belt in the car either. Also, there were no baby seats in the car. It was not the law. So, let me tell you why I started to wear seat belts even before the law came into effect. In Toronto, there is highway called Gardner Express way, it passes through over a river called Humber river. On that bridge there was hump, everybody called it Humber bump. Motorcyclist will speed up when approaches this bump and fly in the air and get a kick out of it. One day I was coming to this bump in my car, my car had a bench seat in front seat and I flew over it. When I landed on the road, I was in the front passenger seat, I just slide over other side. I was not wearing seat belts. So, I had to slide back to drivers' side and grab the wheels while car was still speeding. I could have ended up in a big accident and could have hurt some people. That day onwards I decided to wear seat belts. Now listen to this, when I was in India last time, one of friend send the car to pick me up. So as soon as I sat in the front seat, I wore seat belt. So, the driver told me, sir you don't have to wear seat belt. Only driver has to wear by law. I told him, yes, I have to, whether what is the law says or not, you are wearing it for your own safety. I don't understand the law there, only driver's life is important? Same thing on motor cycle, back seat passenger doesn't have to wear helmets. Hope they changed the law.

Let me add a small story about my first name, which is Inasu. I didn't like this name either. From high school, I was complaining about it to my mother, I want to change my name. My mother told me firmly, Inasu is your grandfather's name, and you are the first grandchild who got that name, you cannot change that name, as long as he is alive. I did not bring it up for few years. One day my sister's girl friend came to our house, and she introduced me to her, this is my brother Inasu. As soon as her friend heard the name, she said, oh what a beautiful name, it is so romantic, sounds Italian. Now this girl is not just any girl, she was a beauty queen, Miss Bangalore, a real knock out. So that day onwards, I never complained about my name. I wonder how that beauty queen looks like now after more than 50 years. Now there are lots of Inasu in the family. Needless to say, my both sons, cut short the last name to "Nadakav". I wish they had not done that.

Toronto was a nice honest city, but boring place compared to Montreal. In the weekends or when we get some time we go there. Montreal was biggest city and financial centre then. When you think about it 1967 EXPO was in Montreal and also1976 OLYMBICS was in Montreal. It is disappointing that Toronto was not able to attract these events even after few attempts. Now Toronto changed quit a bit. Those days even the news paper stands didn't have locks, you just put money and take the paper, no problem. With development lot of things changed. When I came here, there were no CN Tower, Rogers centre, Wonderland, Eaton Centre, None of the tall bank towers, Harbourfront or the other big malls. York Dale, was the only major shopping centre here, that was third biggest mall in the world at that time. Yorkville was a hippy hangout area. Now Yorkville is the most expensive commercial area in Canada. So much has changed here. Harbourfront was full of ware houses and mills. I thought everything is so cheap here. With my salary I could afford almost anything. With $50,000 you can get a beautiful house in expensive area. I bought my first house in 1972, three years after I landed here for $24,000. This was three-bedroom town house with finished basement. Full tank of gas will cost $9.00. My favourite food is egg, which cost 28 cents for a dozen, unbelievable. I loved it. Most of all, I liked the highways here. What a fun to drive here. It is so funny, when I came here, I didn't know there is speed limits. One day I was driving with my friend at reckless speed, he asked me, why are you driving so fast, speed limit is only 60Km. I asked him, what you mean? He said you will get speeding ticket and loose points. Then I was careful, this is long before the police, let me go because of my name. In India, there was no speed limits, then again you cannot speed in India. Cows and everything else on the road will slow you down. You constantly, honk the horn to warn the people to move out of the way. So, you don't have to worry about speeding. I am talking about the situation 50 years ago. Now it is different problem, everybody can afford to buy cars and motor cycles, traffic is so congested, so, you can forget about speeding.

Then in 1972 I decided to get married. I went back to Bangalore, my parents arranged to meet a girl in Kerala. I was driving with my mom, brother and a sister. When we reached a major city on the way, was completely blocked by 10,000 bullock carts. They were on strike. I don't know what was the issue. Mile long cars parked on the road side. I was also on this line. I was looking for ways to get out, otherwise you will end up spending night on the road. Suddenly in my side mirror, I saw a car, few cars behind driving down the slop to a field and started moving forward. I decided to follow him. It was very rough field. Then he crossed small stream may be with 6 inches of water. I crossed it too, there were only two cars on this field. People in other cars on road side may be wondered what is wrong with these guys. Anyway, he stopped the car in front of me, so I got out too, asked me where are you going, I told him I have to get out of this mess, how can you help us. He said follow him. We reached in front of huge mansion with 8 car garages. Apparently, he is the grandson of one of India's richest people. He let me park the car in one of the garages. Took us to a hotel, people are crowded in lawn of the hotel to get room, it was full. He said he will be back soon and comes back with key to private villa and told us he will come at midnight to take us to railway station. We did all this by walking because nothing is moving in the city due to strike. As promised, he came at midnight, same story in the railway station, he went to see station master and comes back with tickets. Unfortunately, with influence you can get things done in India while others suffer. Anyway, I went to meet my wife and marriage was arranged. Within two weeks we came back to Toronto.

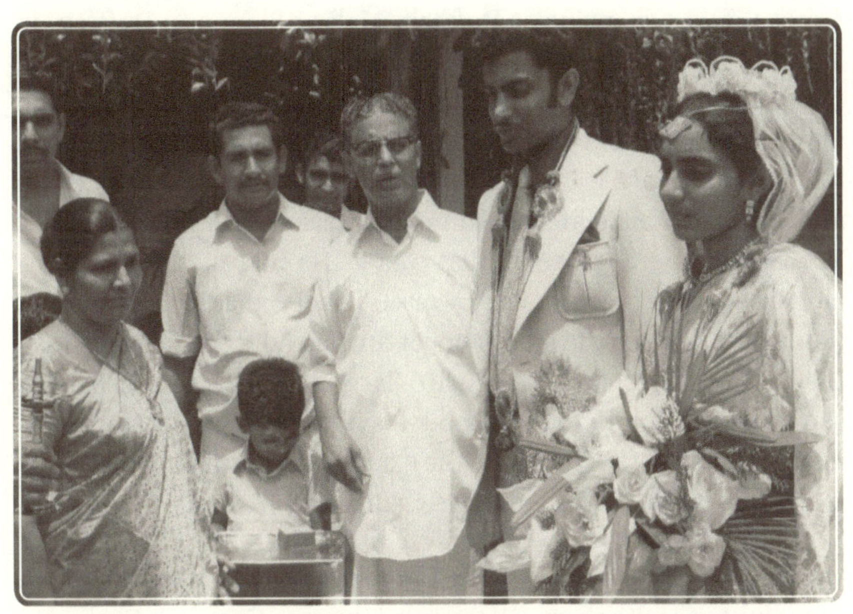

My wedding

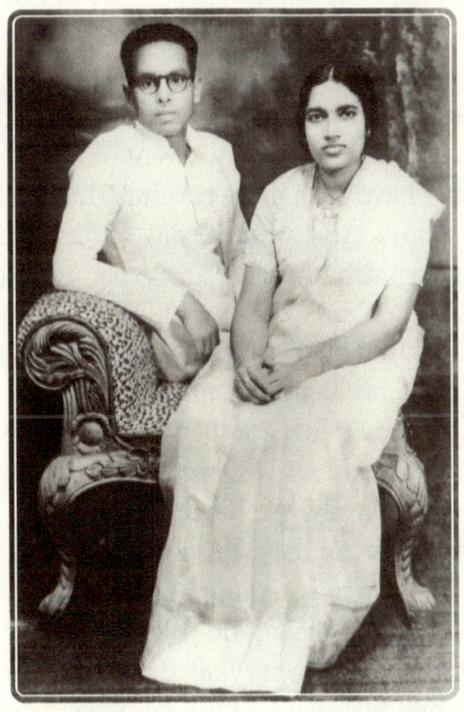

My wife's parents

In 1974, I was shopping at Dufferin Mall at Bloor and Dufferin in Toronto. Then a sign on the door saying Canadian Citizen ship office. I walked in, a guy was sitting there with his legs on the table and almost sleeping. He woke up and asked me what Can I do for you. I said I want to take Canadian Citizenship. He asked me to sit down and gave me a bible and asked me to swear your loyalty to queen. Then asked me to pay $12, that was it. He told me I will get my citizenship card in two weeks by mail. To get Canadian Citizenship, now a days, you have to study about Canada and write an exam, then there is swearing in ceremony with a large group, who are also doing same thing. I think, there is a book available to help you to learn about Canada before you write the exam. I wonder if anybody really fail at this exam. How times have changed.

Our children both boys were born in 1974 and 1977. It was lot of fun spending time with them. We travelled through Canadian Rockies to west coast, Disney world, and East coast. We drove through Germany, France, Switzerland, Italy and Austria. The boys and myself taken Martial arts classes together. The instructor used to think we are three brothers. Then enjoyed bicycling with them. Some times we carry too far and wonder how do we get back that distance. One time my younger son was at young age, we went too far and he started to throw up, I should have been more careful. They both served in the church as server boys. All I want to say, generally they were good boys didn't give me much trouble. I am so happy with them.

Let me tell you what happened in one of our trips, we could have all been killed in an accident, but miraculously escaped. We were returning from Florida, with another family after visiting Disney World and other attractions. We were all in a custom-built van belongs to the other family. We have two boys and they have two boys. Usually when I am in the car, I don't let anybody else drive no matter how far we have to go. That particular trip, we stayed extra one day to see space shuttle takes off. We both had to report to work the following day and it was very long drive through night. So, I let my friend drive for a little while. Both our wives were sitting in the second-row seats and all four boys were sleeping in the custom-made bed in the back. Basically, everybody in the van was sleeping, soon I will find out that includes the driver. I thought myself to take a short nap, thinking soon I have to drive all the way back. This was also very unusual for me to sleep, when somebody else drives. While I am sleeping, I was feeling something was choking me, I could not breathe, some thing in white colour, in other words it was trying to wake me up. When I opened my eyes, my first thought was my God it was too late for all of us: we were heading down the hill straight to a trailer truck. When I glanced at the driver, he was sleeping at the wheel with cruise control set at 70 Miles per hour I shouted his name and with my left hand turned the wheel and avoided the truck, our side mirror only hit the truck. Driver wakes up and asking what happened, we didn't even stop, he was all shaken didn't utter one word. Within ten minutes, I took over from him. We couldn't stop anywhere to change places for ten minutes. I tell you that was the longest ten minutes in my life. This was all happened in few seconds. So, here is the question, how can I turn the wheels within seconds on custom built van, especially some one also holding the steering wheel. Also, there is big console between our seats. I would say whatever woke me up helped to turn the wheels also. You can call it guardian angel or God, but some super natural power helped me, maybe it was not our time yet to die that night. It was purely a miracle.

While I am talking about miracles, I like to share one more incident, I will call another miracle. The year was 1979, when my company Chrysler was almost bankrupt. We all took a salary cut and frozen our salary for three years to save Chrysler. I was the only member working in the family. To make things worse, my mortgage rate went up to 19.5%. Some people with bad credit was paying up to 24%. I could not carry on, but I never missed one payment in my life so far. I took loans from everywhere, even took all the money out of my credit cards. I was at end of my rope. I was out of money to pay my next mortgage payment remember buying an instant lottery ticket during lunch break, but no luck. Finally, I accepted the fact that I may lose the house. I need $1,800 for the payment. I was ashamed to ask money from my friends. I was back at my work place. Suddenly my supervisor called me and told that, there was a phone call for me. I picked up the phone and it was lawyers secretary, she told me that she was on vacation, but there is a$1,800 cheque is sitting here on your name and explained, this was the adjustment from mortgage commission when I switched mortgage to another company. I couldn't believe my ears, I asked her can you repeat what you said. She repeated and told me that; she will mail it. I said no, I am coming there to collect it. So, I asked permission to leave the work and got the cheque and I went to straight to my bank and made the payment. Within a month got promoted as supervisor, then things started to turn around. Later on, I was attending Dale Carnegie course and everyone has to give a speech from your own experience. So, I spoke about what happened to me and I won the price for my speech.

So, a short period I was with so many other people were laid off from Chrysler. Immediately I was looking for another job. I saw this nice-looking building and walked in, asked the receptionist, what you do here. She told me we make pace makers for the heart. Company is Medtronic leading manufacture of heart pace makers. So, I told her, then you may not need me with my background in automotive business. She insisted me to leave my resume anyway. Before I reached home, I got a call from Engineering manager of Medtronic to come back for an interview. At interview, he asked me if I can work there on contract for two months as an engineering assistant. So, I accepted the job, to my surprise I was able to make major improvements there. I made where they use three people, changed to one-person operation by designing special tools. They asked me to stay longer. Mean while Chrysler called me back, so I was doing two jobs same time, finally Chrysler got so busy under Iacocca. So, I said good bye to Medtronic after 10 months working there. Medtronic is a fantastic company to work for. In appreciation, they gave me a letter for my contribution, I still cherish that letter.

Meanwhile at Chrysler I was working with forty Canadian senior skilled tool & die makers. Soon management asked me if I want to be supervisor of this group. I told them, let me think about. I thought many things, will they give me hard time because they all are senior to me and worried about discrimination. Apparently, I was in short list of two other seniors. One from Czechoslovak and other from Switzerland. Gentleman from Czechoslovak an excellent guy and well respected, he told the management, that George will be better supervisor than him. Most of the people call me George, which is my middle name. So, one week later they came to me again and asked me to make up my mind. They told me clearly, they want me to take the job. So, I accepted. Normally all the supervisors go for two weeks training in the head office. They didn't send me for few weeks, so I asked them when I am not going for the training. Manager told me you don't need any training. That was my very proud moment.

During my tenure as supervisor, I did many improvements and reduced skilled labour even though production was doubled. This plant where I worked was the biggest and most cost-efficient piston manufacturer in the world, we produced pistons even for General Motors. 19 million pistons we used to make per year. We had developed in house mechanical robots and used to fully automated cells. Nobody in the world could touch us. We were so cost efficient. This is before real programable robots came. we had only 16 pressure diecasting machines that increased to 32 machines. What I did, I did not lay off anybody instead, when somebody retired or quit, I did not replace them. Finally, number of tool makers reduced to 27 from 40. This was huge savings. To achieve that I have to make so many improvements, too many to mention here. Also motivate the employees and getting them involved in operation. It is funny, before when we get visitors from the head office, we tried to avoid the skilled labour section to hide deficiencies. After the improvements, that department became pride of our company. I made them give presentations by the employees to visitors. Visitors commented about the enthusiasm and pride of that department.

After couple of years, they asked me to join engineering team. They put me in charge of piston division. I really did good job, I brought down scrap from 15% to almost zero. I brought many innovations and made major changes to increase production and quality and cut the cost. Every month, I was cost cutting champion. Out of all these promotions, I most enjoyed looking after piston engineering. When I go home, I get real satisfaction. I feel like I did something great today. Chrysler recognized me by presenting: Outstanding Achievement Award. This award is top award from our group. Which consists of 16 divisions spread across North America.

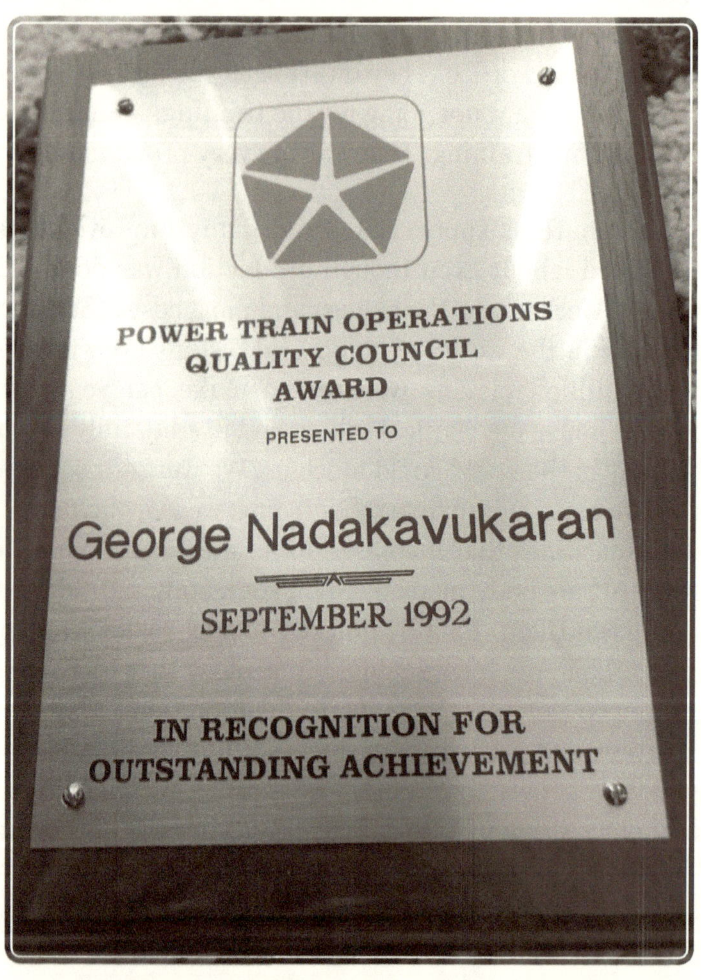

Outstanding achievement award from Chrysler

Soon more and more responsibilities were coming to my shoulder, promoted to Engineering supervisor. There I was heading Tool room with 27 skilled craftsman, designers, Piston, Master brake cylinders and machining. I was also in charge of buying new equipments and writing projects and specifications. I hired all graduate engineers to train them as Tooling and Process engineers. During this time, I had to visit most of Chrysler plants including There was an issue between our plant and Mexico plant. Even though both are Chrysler plants, we operated separately. If one makes a mistake there is no forgiveness. When I was there, I resolved this issue on my very first visit. So, the General Manager from Mexico plant called my General Manager to send George here every 3 months, then we wouldn't have no problems. So, I used to go there every 3 months. Mexicans loved me, they thought I am also a Mexican. In the street they come and talk to me in Spanish, when I say I am not Mexican, they will say you look like us and you have mustache. Once I met an engineer in Chrysler plant his name spelled Jesus. So, I called him Jesus, he said Jesus is up there, I am Hesus (this is how they pronounce Jesus in Mexico). They also told me one of their old kings' name is something like my last name, so that was another reason they were showing respect to me. Let me tell you about my first visit to Mexico, I travelled with one of the quality engineers with me. Driver who picked us from the airport is craziest guy I have ever seen. I am not kidding, he was driving at 200km, in the rain. I really thought I was going to die that day; I was so tired and sleepy. But I don't want to sleep, because I thought, if I am going to die, I want to see, my death. Isn't it a crazy thought? Then I noticed my friend who was sitting in front was not wearing seat belt. I asked him put your seat belt on, you know what he said. I don't want to insult the driver now wearing seat belt. I ordered him, put it on. I thought about the Delhi driver who picked me from airport and took me to the hotel. I start to wonder between these two drivers who is most dangerous? Finally reached at the plant and told the general manager, give us another driver when we go back. One day, I was travelling with this General Manager and I was sitting in the back seat. I saw base ball bat lying on the floor. I asked him, oh do you play base ball. He laughed and told me, no George, that is for another purpose. If some accident or mishap happened in the road, you don't get out just like that, you take the bat with you, you have to show who is in charge here, otherwise they will be all over you, if they talk louder and shouting at you, you have to be even more louder and get angry with them. So, you have to learn all these tricks when you are visiting new places. I don't guarantee, this works all the time. So, don't blame me when it goes against you.

Now my children grown up and it was time to join university. My eldest son said, he wants go for medicine in Hungary, it was very expensive, my wife was not working. Why Hungary, you might ask. He didn't have high marks to get onto Toronto University. It was easier to get into Hungary, all taught in English language and recognized in North America. My second son was doing law in Hamilton ON, staying in the hostel. After one year he came to me asked me, if he can also go for medicine in Hungary. I could not really afford one son in medicine, when the second son also asked me to go there, my heart stopped, but I didn't want disappoint him, I told him sure, I will manage somehow.

I got one more promotion as Engineering Manager in Chrysler, I was role model in Chrysler, that is top position you get for your overall performance, which includes risk taking, innovation, leadership, cost cutting, projects completion on time and evaluation from other departments, it is not easy to get this position. You have to be perfect in everything. Now as a Manager, you do more administrative work than technical, but I still get involved with everything, still I was solving lot of technical problems. I loved to work there. I am eligible for 5 weeks vacation yearly. Most of the years, I won't take my full vacation and you cannot accumulate either. So, I just loose my vacation. By 5:30 AM, I am in my office, otherwise after 7:30AM, I have to attend all five department meetings. I hated unnecessary meetings. For example, we used to have production meeting in the morning and afternoon. I thought afternoon meeting was total waste of time. So new General Manger was chairing afternoon meeting. At end of the meeting, he asked let us go around the table, if anybody has anything to say. It came to my turn, so I asked do we really need this meeting. Everybody stunned and my immediate boss, banged on the table and told, until we get out of the woods, we need this meeting. I told, if we sit here, we never going to get out of the woods. He didn't like that very much, but General Manger asked the rest any comments, nobody said anything. So General Manager, said there won't be any more afternoon production meetings, unless there is a special need. And there was no special need until I left Chrysler. My boss told me afterwards, everybody trying to score with new General Manager. I told him, I am not, I would rather go down and help the plant rather than sitting here, tying up 14 people. It was total waste of time. He didn't say anything back.

I always want to start my meetings on time and finish on time. One time, my meeting was over as usual on time, but my boss said let us go around the table to see if anyone has anything to say. I said no, meeting is over. Everybody was look at me, this is a new boss. So afterwards, I went to see my boss and told him, if I didn't stop the meeting, I will be late for another meeting, where people are waiting. He told, me George you did the right thing. Told me don't be afraid to speak up.

Another time, we were going to award a big project worth millions of dollars. At the award meeting, we were 15 of in the room. I know it was going to be big mistake, I know I am the only on in the room opposed to the idea, there were others, but they don't want to go against the boss. Half way in the meeting, I thought myself I have to stop this somehow, big mistake if we do proceed with this plan. So, I asked my boss, can we step out for 10 minutes. So, he came out and told everybody take a break for ten minutes. I got him in the office and locked the door and explained to him, why the proposal won't work. It will be huge mistake if we proceed with this plan, and proved him why, I was pleasantly surprised when he said suddenly, that we will go with your proposal. He dismissed the meeting and told everybody what we are going to do. He never stopped thanking me to pull him out of the meeting and help him make that wise decision. My proposal worked like a charm, without any hiccups and we had very successful launch

At the same time, I was drowning in debts, by supporting with one income. I was borrowing from all credit cards and taking equity from house, eventually sold first house. Then another company offered me even higher salary job, I did not apply for the job. Still I didn't want to leave Chrysler. Who will leave at that position? It was my home. Then I thought, it is God given, with that job and early retirement from Chrysler, with combined income I can pull through. Long term it was a loss, because I won't get full pension. Normally when somebody take early retirement or leave Chrysler, you are not allowed to go back to your desk, you have to leave the plant. Chrysler thought I would never leave and they don't want to make me to take Early retirement. In case I do, they had special permission to keep me for another 6 months. I decided to take early retirement and last minute, I walked in Human Resources office and told that I am taking the package. He was shocked but understood my predicament and told me about six months permission and tried to keep me for six more months, but I stayed one more month to help and left Chrysler, it was biggest decision I made in my life. My heart was broken. So, after one month, my friends asked me so George, are you going to take some time off before I join Orlick Industries where my new job waiting for me. I said sure I am taking off Saturday and Sunday, the weekend. I was kind of workaholic. I am not sure it is good or bad

Life outside Chrysler

I decided to take the job offer from Orlick Industries as key Account Manger for Honda and other automotive plants. During this time, I travelled, quite often to Honda head office in Ohio and other plants. I always take my car and I end up lot of speeding tickets and I lost 9 points for speeding, that is when government call you for an interview to question, why I should have license. So, I had interview with a lady, she told me why I am there and she knows my past record, didn't have any accidents or anything and told me we all speed little bit, but I don't want to see you again in 5 years. So, I told her, I don't want to see again also. So, she jokingly told me get out of my office, that was the interview. I am glad to say, I don't have any points, I am clean now.

Honda operates, their companies totally different, I learned lot from them and big three should also learn. I have such a respect for them. I have so much to write about it. I don't want to bore you with all these details. At Orlick industries, pay was good plus I was getting pension from Chrysler, so I was able to make payments. I was doing great, then I made a mistake joining a group to start Die Casting plants in Canada, States and even far East. I was offered a position as vice president and equal partnership without investing my own money. We build up two plants, one in Cape Breton Nova Scotia and one in Mississauga. And bought one plant in St Catharines, ON. It was too ambitious in short period with out enough funds. Finance was not in my control, I don't want to go into details, let us say, all these companies closed down within two years. It was my darkest days of my life. I must say something, during this time I travelled extensively to far east and met very important people. We visited Thailand, Indonesia, Singapore, Malesia and Japan. In States we were invited to start up die casting plants. I met even Governor of Mississippi. and had lunch with him in Toronto. I want to say something what happened in Indonesia. The country was run under dictatorship of Sukarno, almost everything was controlled by his family, some how I was not very comfortable there, you can say I got bad vibes. So, I told my company chairman, I am not very comfortable here, let us get out of here, I told him I am not interested to do business here. I also told him actually it was a bet, that this government will come down within three months. He told me, it never is going to happen and told me, the president has full support of the army. I repeated three months and students is going to bring the government down. My chairman personally knows the second man in command. He knows what he is talking about. Can you imagine his shock in three months Government was brought down by students? He couldn't believe it, he told me I could have made lot of money by betting this. Anyway, I thought I should share this event.

My boys are in still studying medicine in Europe, expense was still growing. Then I got a job as consultant for Magna, this was a contract job for one year. Magna is the biggest Automobile parts company in the world. I was doing great there. I was driving between two Magna plant everyday. One is very large new plant with lots of capacity and other one is older plant. Older plant was on lease, new one owned by Magna. I suggested why don't move everything to new facility and shut down the old plant. That is exactly what happened, even though, it was end of my career there. It was good decision for Magna. Then I helped a friend of mine to set up a die casting plant. It was just a small plant. I was involved in the initial stage only. After that, I took license in Real Estate and worked for two years. It was not for me, plus I started to travel, so it didn't work out very well. I started boutique store in historical district in Unionville ON, I had that for two years, before closing it down. To make things worse, I got a letter from Govt, stating I owe $560,000 for tax payment for the company we were running. It also says, even though you were not responsible for finances as director what did you do to prevent problems. I thought I had destroyed all the papers about this company, yet I decided to go down to the locker room to see if any shred of evidence there about this company. There was yellow envelope, and in it there was everything I needed. I have done everything by book. There were letters warning the chairman about tax issues and problems facing this company. There were meeting minutes and everything I needed. I gave this to my accountant and he submitted to the Government, and they let me go without charging me any fine. They found; I was innocent.

By this time my children graduated from medical college. I think I mentioned earlier that, they studied in Hungary. Most of the students were from USA, Canada, Norway and Israel. After graduation, they still have to write exams US Emilie step one, two and three to get admission as residents in USA. They didn't want to work in Canada. This process was also very expensive. There are exam fees and lawyers fee. They both got residency in America. My eldest got in Cincinnati, Ohio and younger son got in Rochester, NY. After residency program, my oldest son decided to stay in Cincinnati and younger one moved to Mooresville, NC. I was little bit sad, because I was hoping they will work in Canada, close to me. When I asked them why are you going to states, they asked me dad, you left your parents and came all the way here to Canada, and we are still in the same continent and you can easily visit us. I didn't have anything to say.

During residency program, they both met their life partners, and told me what was going on. I didn't have any problems with that. I didn't have to arrange their marriage. Only advised them this is one of the most important decision in your life, you are doctors' money won't be the problem, if you don't have good partner, that money cannot buy any happiness, so use your head before, falling in love. So, look for positive person and non complainers. My eldest son met a girl who is also doctor, were born in Canada whose, parents are from India. My second son met a girl who is also a doctor, came from India to do residency in the same hospital, where my second son works. My first son marriage was a destination wedding In Santiago,

California. Originally planned in Florida, then somebody advised us that it is hurricane season not a good idea to have wedding in East Coast. It was a wise decision, sure enough Katrina hit Florida same time as my son's wedding. Few of my friends couldn't attend the wedding because of this storm. Wedding was great, still lot of people came some as far as Australia. A year after my second son wants to get married. He wants his destination wedding done in Kerala, India. Again, similar problems happened there. We booked banquet hall for wedding in Trichur without realizing there is major festival happening there on that day. Million people comes to the festival. Most of the roads will be blocked. So, we shifted the wedding to Kochi at Taj Hotel. It was a grand wedding. Indian weddings are very big. My eldest son and his wife, have four children, two of them are twins. Out of four children one is a girl. My second son and his wife have two children, one boy and a girl. So, we have six grand children. My youngest grand child was born on my 75th birthday. You cannot ask better gift than that. If I have to visit my eldest son and family, I have to drive 800 km to Cincinnati and to visit my second son and his family, I have to drive 1,200km. I love driving, so that is not a problem. I can fly to these places, but that is too boring for me.

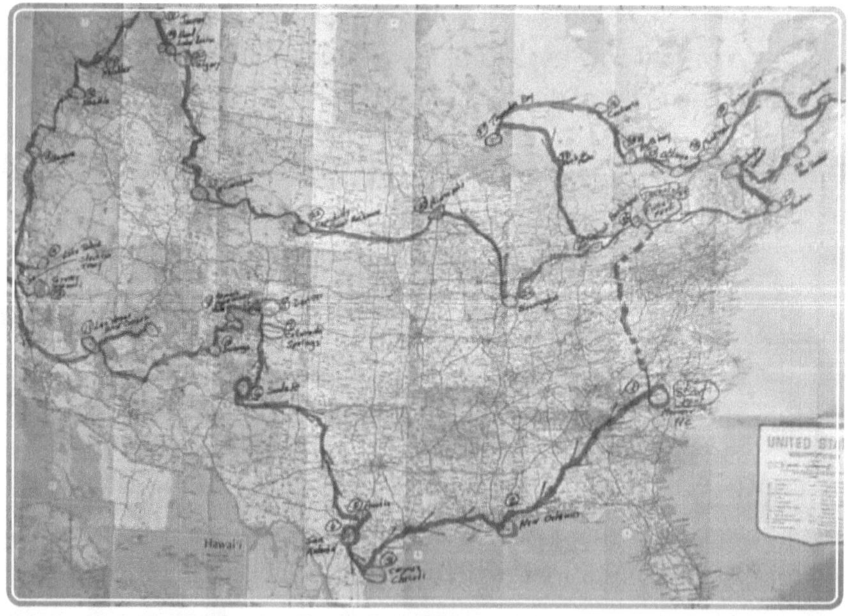

Speaking of driving, I recently completed 26,000 km mega trip across North America by myself. It was amazing experience. I drove through all kind of weather. I went through floods, high mountain passes, deserts, fog and snow storms. The scenery was spectacular. I started from Mooresville, North Carolina and end up in Toronto. On the way, drove through Colorado Rockies, pacific highway to Canadian Rockies to East coast to Boston and then to Cape Breton, Nova Scotia. I was Criss crossing border few times. There is so much to see in Canada and USA, you can travel your life time still you won't be to see everything. You have travel different seasons also to see the beauty I was trying to get into Guinness book of world records, but I was supped to inform them before I started the trip. Anyway, I just published a book about this mega trip. It is called "26,000 KM Mega Road Trip by Solo Driver" If you are interested it is available in Amazon, Kindle and Barns and Noble. Now I am already planning my next mega trip. If it is God's will, I plan to drive from Toronto to Alaska. It is little bit ambitious trip, considering the terrain and weather. Some other people shown interest to go with me. Even if they don't come, I will do it myself.

My Current Situation

As I mentioned, in the beginning, I am 75 years old and 50 years in Canada. I came here in 1969, I cannot complain much, I was able to find jobs immediately in my profession. Married in 1972 and have two sons, I wrote about them earlier so, I am not repeating about their careers.

I liked to keep busy myself. I don't mind taking up another job. As a matter of fact, an offer came from biggest automobile parts manufacture to set up a plant in States. I jumped and took that offer. This could have been a challenging job at my age. Then after consulting with my children and decided not to take that job. So that is end of my career. Now I am trying to relax at home and travel little bit. Most of all I enjoy visiting my grand children. It is too bad they live in States. I wish they were closer. I was much farther away from my parents, so I cannot complain.

Looking Back

ow, I am here for last 50 years. So, what happened to my rest of siblings or the family I left behind. They all visited me few times and then returned home. Someone may ask, how come they are not settling here. This may surprise many people. They are all living good life there and I must say, even better than me. India is not same as people think or read in the papers. Of course, there are lot of poverty. But do you know 31 million people coming out of poverty every year. That is equivalent to one Canada growing inside India every year. Can you imagine that. India is very rich country; people can afford cars and all the luxuries. Recently I read in the paper, Bangalore is the most congested city in the world. When I was there last time, I read in seven-month period, they sold 93,000 cars and 350,000 motor cycles in Bangalore alone. Now tell me which city sells that many cars. You will see more luxury cars there than in Toronto. I am talking about not just Mercedes and BMW, people driving Rolls Royce and other luxury models and sports cars. In my small town, a business man own 3 brand new Rolls Royce. I like to add an interesting story about Rolls Royce, During British rule an Indian Maharaja. Went to buy a Rolls Royce, in casual dress. They won't sell the car to him, So, actually they insulted him in a revenge, he ordered 6 luxury Rolls Royce to haul the garbage, to insult the company. So, later they send an apology letter to him. My point is this, there are lot of poverty there, I admit lot of things has to change. But things are happening there. Middle class is growing and population is very young, you will see lot of changes coming there.

Education standards are much higher in my opinion. You must have heard about famous institutes like IIT, IAM, and Indian Institute of science, can easily compete with any other top universities of the world. It is harder in get into IIT than MIT. It is not coincidence, people were graduated from here, running the largest corporations in the world. I will list some of them below. I am talking about, Google, Microsoft, IBM, Adobe, Nokia, Pepsi Cola to name a few. People of Indian Origin ran City Bank, Deutsche Bank and Oracle and so many other large corporations. I know you will hear more and more about such things. India is not same, when I left there. India got independence only in 1947, that is just 73 years. During this time India become one of the strongest economies. They excel in every field including space.

Every year I go and visit my family there. Every time I go there, I have fantastic time. I see the energy in young people. I am sure we will see lot of things coming out of India and including some large companies which are start ups now. Indian IT industry is well known. Let us wait and see. Sometime I wish I was part of this tremendous energy; I wish all the best to young peoples of India.

Advice to new immigrants

I wish you all very best this country can offer. Canada is very beautiful and tolerant country. Some people have difficult time adjusting here and finding jobs. You will wonder if you made the right decision immigrating to Canada. Lot of people had this concern. I will tell you in couple of years or sooner, you will say it is the best decision you ever made coming here. Here lot of things going for you. Sooner you get engaged here is better for you. For that what I mean, you have to show confidence and eagerness, when you look for jobs. Of course, If you can get job in your own field it is better, but if you didn't get it, you have to start somewhere. Don't accept the fact, that you don't have Canadian experience. That is just an excuse. If I were you, if somebody told me I don't have Canadian experience, I will ask sir can you explain what is Canadian experience. We are all doing the same jobs. Need some adjusting to do. That is all. As a matter of fact, when I came here, I found, Canada was so backward from what I have seen in India where I studied. I started working in my profession very next day. Don't be afraid, show your attitude, confidence, determination and eagerness. When I interview applicants, I don't check their qualifications first. I will be more interested in their attitude. They have to have confidences to hire you, don't fall for Canadian experience. You have to show them you can do the job. Read about this company before you go for interview. These days everything is available in Google. I will write below about a program to help new immigrants when I was at Chrysler.

I was engineering manager at Chrysler plant in Toronto. I was working with Board of education to help to get jobs for new engineers. I dealt mostly with engineers, because that was my department. We took engineers for a three-month period, Chrysler didn't pay any salary, but only Transit monthly pass. Now this was excellent program. This was a win win situation, During the three-month period, I was able to see some good engineers and if there were a vacancy, I will hire them. If I don't have a vacancy, I will check with our suppliers to see if they are hiring and will recommend them. For engineers they can add Chrysler experience in the resume and give my name as reference. When the company calls me, I will tell my honest opinion. Once I took an engineer who had PHD in metallurgy, he was determined to get permanent job in Chrysler. So, he asked me after his three months, if he can stay another three months without pay and work as production worker. I let him do that and a vacancy came engineering during the second three months period and I hired him permanently. I had few people like that. So, check with Board of education if that program still available.

My Thoughts on General Subjects

Toronto was a peaceful place, now everyday we are hearing about a shooting in different parts of the city. Lot of guns are smuggled to the city. In my opinion, if you shoot somebody, whether he dies or not, he should be charged for murder not attempted murder. His intention was to kill. He may be a lousy shot; in my opinion he should be charged for murder. Shooting is justified only in self defence situation.

If anybody harm or kill a policeman, punishment must be severe, at the same time a policeman harm or kill an innocent man, punishment must be even more severe, not paid suspension leave.

Human trafficking is worse crime than murder, Law should change and make it capitol punishment

I wish Canada will have a flat tax system based on percentage of income. That is most fair system. Hong Kong has 15% flat tax for everybody, in Canada the percentage may be different to work. So, the higher income people pay higher tax and lower income people pay lesser tax. Everybody pays same percentage. No loop holes to claim back taxes. I remember a politician in Canada suggested this. Life will be lot simpler and Govt will get enough money to run the country.

Balancing the budget must be a law. We are spending so much money on interest to maintain the debts.

Monarchy should be abolished in Canada. In Canada we have to consider French Canada and English Canada, I don't understand, why French Canadians should take allegiances to English Monarch. I don't thing it is good for the unity of Canada. It will be sad to see If Canada get separated into two countries.

I believe, there should be an age limit to run for political office, like prime minister, supreme court justice or president if there is one. May be a maximum age of 75.

It is my opinion, major issues like separation of the country, should be decided on 2/3rd majority and not based on simple majority.

These are few of my thoughts, I am not saying it is right or wrong, I am just expressing my opinions.

I wish all new immigrants, peaceful, healthy and prosperous life in Canada. You made a wise decision. It is up to you make it a beautiful life for you and your family. You have to be flexible and willing to change and change your direction. Most importantly remember, your attitude is more important than your qualifications and you have to believe in yourself. Don't give up hope. I wish you all the best, Canada can offer.

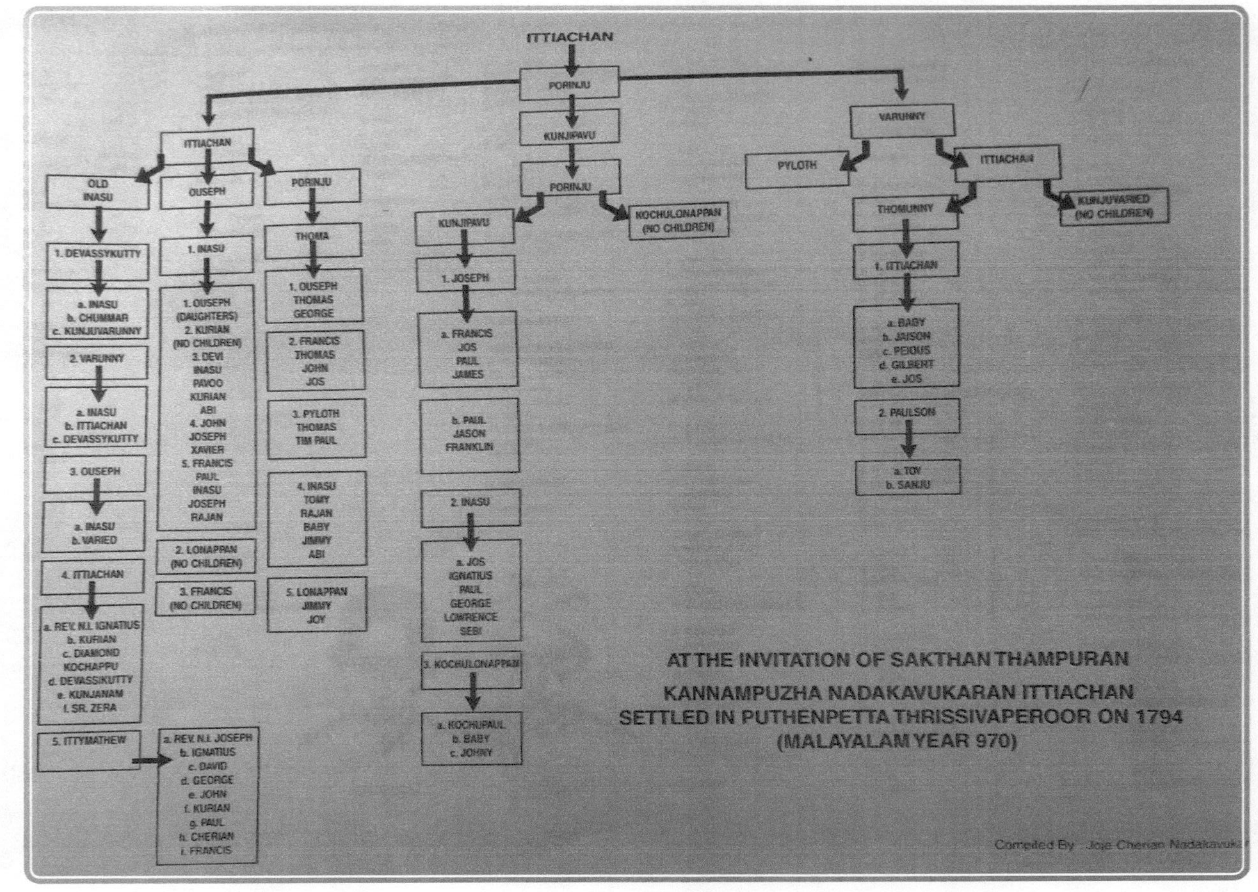

ITTIACHAN
PORINJU

ITTIACHAN
KUNJIPAVU
VARUHNY

OLD INASU
OUSEPH
PORINJU

PYLOTH
ITTIACHAN
KUNJUVARIED (NO CHILDREN)

1. DEVASSYKUTTY
a. INASU
b. CHUMMAR
c. KUNJUVARUNNY

2. VARUNNY
a. INASU
b. ITTIACHAN
c. DEVASSYKUTTY

3. OUSEPH
a. INASU
b. VARIED

4. ITTIACHAN
a. REV. N.I. IGNATIUS
b. KURIAN
c. DIAMOND KOCHAPPU
d. DEVASSIKUTTY
e. KUNJANAM
f. SR. ZERA

5. ITTYMATHEW
a. REV. N.I. JOSEPH
b. IGNATIUS
c. DAVID
d. GEORGE
e. JOHN
f. KURIAN
g. PAUL
h. CHERIAN
i. FRANCIS

1. INASU
1. OUSEPH (DAUGHTERS)
2. KURIAN (NO CHILDREN)
3. DEVI INASU PAVOO KURIAN ABI
4. JOHN JOSEPH XAVIER
5. FRANCIS PAUL INASU JOSEPH RAJAN
2. LONAPPAN (NO CHILDREN)
3. FRANCIS (NO CHILDREN)

THOMA
1. OUSEPH THOMAS GEORGE
2. FRANCIS THOMAS JOHN JOS
3. PYLOTH THOMAS TIM PAUL
4. INASU TOMY RAJAN BABY JIMMY ABI
5. LONAPPAN JIMMY JOY

KUNJIPAVU
PORINJU
KOCHULONAPPAN (NO CHILDREN)

1. JOSEPH
a. FRANCIS JOS PAUL JAMES
b. PAUL JASON FRANKLIN
2. INASU
a. JOS IGNATIUS PAUL GEORGE LOWRENCE SEBI
3. KOCHULONAPPAN
a. KOCHUPAUL
b. BABY
c. JOHNY

THOMUNNY
1. ITTIACHAN
a. BABY
b. JAISON
c. PEIOUS
d. GILBERT
e. JOS
2. PAULSON
a. TOY
b. SANJU

AT THE INVITATION OF SAKTHAN THAMPURAN
KANNAMPUZHA NADAKAVUKARAN ITTIACHAN
SETTLED IN PUTHENPETTA THRISSIVAPEROOR ON 1794
(MALAYALAM YEAR 970)

Compiled By : Jose Cherian Nadakavukaran

KANNAMPUZHA NADAKAVUKARAN ITTIACHAN INASU (OLD INASU) WIFE : MARIAM CHERPUKARAN

DEVASSYKUTTY
WIFE : CHERUCHI
CHITTILAPPILLY

1. INASU
a. DEVASSYKUTTY
INASU:- GEORGE:-
DAVIS, FRANCIS SAJIN, SANJU

b. JOSUMER
NETTO, JETTO

2. CHUMMAR
a. JOSEPH
SIMON:-
JOSEPH, MARIYA
TONY, GEORGE

b. DAVIS
SIMON:-VISHION
SANTHOSH:-
DAVIS, VERGHESE
SABU:- RITTU

c. KURIAN
PEARL, WINCY
VIGI, SHAJI

d. CHUMMAR
SIMON:- ROHAN
ZAVI, SEEMA

3. KUNJUVARUNNY
(DAUGHTERS)

4. ELIYAKUTTY
W/O. ITTOOP
PULIKKEN

5. KOCHUMARIYAM
W/O. KOCHANTHONY
KALLIYATH

VARUNNY
WIFE :
1. ACHAI, KODANKANDATH
2. KUNJETHY, NELLISSERY

1. INASU
a. VARUNNY
IGNATIUS:-
ANU, ANI,

VARGHESE:-
BIBIN, PINKY,
JOS:-THEJUS

2. ITTIACHAN
a. JOSE:-
SANTHOSH
SANJAY
b. GEORGE:-
BIJOY
c. INASU:-
TITTY, BOBBY
d. DAVID:-
ITSON, TREESA
e. LAZERUS

3. DEVASSYKUTTY
a. GEORGE:-
DAVIS, SEETHAL
b. THOMAS:- DAVID
c. INASU:- ANILS
d. ITTIACHAN
e. JOS:-
RICHE, RIYA
f. PHILOMINA

4. ITTIANAM
CHAKOLA HOUSE

5. THANDAMMA
EDATHURUTHIKKARAN

6. ROSY
MANJIYIL

OUSEPH
WIFE : KUNJETHY
CHITTILAPPILLY

1. INASU
a. OUSEPH
INASU:-
JOSEPH, MARIYA,
SUSAN

2. VAREED
a. JOS
b. BABY:-
SABU, SIMMI

ITTIACHAN
WIFE : KUNJANAM CHANDY
THRESSIAMMA
CHEMBUKAVU

1. REV. N.I. IGNATIUS
a. DAVID

2. KURIAN
a. JIMMY
b. SUNNY:- KURIAN
c. IGNATIUS:- KURIAN

3. DIAMOND KOCHAPPU
(DAUGHTER)

4. KATHERINE
W/O. VAREED MANJILA

5. DEVASSYKUTTY
a. JOY:-
WINI, SONIYA, ANTONY
b. IGNATIUS:-
DAVID, JOSEPH
c. KURIAN:-
SAINA, SANJU
d. ALFY:-
CHINNU, FREDY, FRANKY
e. ANTO:-
KEVIN

6. KUNJANAM

7. SR. ZERA

ITTYMATHEW
WIFE : ROSA CHAKOLA

1. REV. N.I. JOSEPH
a. MATHEW
b. JOHN

2. MARIYAM
W/O. DEVASSY
CHAMMANAM

3. KUNJETHY
W/O. REV. PAULOSE
KONIKKARA

4. IGNATIUS
a. ITTYMATHEW:-
IGNATIUS, MATHEW
b. JOS:-
IGNATIUS, MATHEW,
DEEPA
c. JOHN:-
CICILYMARY,
IGNATIUS
d. BOBBY:-
MARIYA, IGNATIUS

5. ELIAKUTTY
W/O. JOSEPH THATTIL

6. DAVID
a. ITTYMATHEW
b. MOHAN:-
YADAV
c. ABL-
MARIS, ANTONY
d. ROSAKUTTY
e. RAJAMMA

7. SARA
W/O. GEORGE IMMATTY

8. GEORGE
a. MATHEW:-
GEORGE, MATHEW
b. INASU:-
SANJAY, SUNIL
c. JOS:-
NITHIN

9. ROSAKUTTY
W/O. KURIAN CHANDY

10. JOHN

KUNJETHY
W/O. KUNJAPPU
LONA DEVASSY

1. ANTONY
a. LONAPPAN
b. VARGHESE

2. INASU

3. JOSEPH
a. INNI
b. DEVASSY
c. ANTONY

4. MATHEW
a. DEVASSY
b. PAUL
c. FRANCIS

5. MARIYAM
MECHERY
ERINJERY

6. ACHUNNY
W/O. KOOLA RAPPAI PYLOTH

7. ELYA

11. KURIAN
a. ITTYMATHEW:-
EUGIN, NEETHU
b. JOHN:-
LIYA, NIYA
c. JOJU

12. PAUL
a. SEBY:-
JOSEPH PAUL
b. ABI
c. JOHN

13. CHERIAN
a. SHAJI:-
RICHIE
b. JOJE:-
CHERIN, JOHN

14. FRANCIS
a. ITTYMATHEW:-
RIYA, RYAN
b. ANTONY:-
ELZA
c. JOHN

ROSA
W/O. PALLAN OUSEPH

1. ANTHONYKUTTY
a. JOSE
b. SUNNY
c. JOY
d. BABY

2. INASU
a. JOSE
b. ANTHONYKUTTY

3. GEORGE
a. BOBBY
b. ROSILY
c. ALICE
d. THANKAMMA
e. SUNNY

4. OUSEPH
a. JOSE
b. MERCY
c. THRESSIA

5. DEVASSYKUTTY
a. JOSE
b. JOHNSON
c. BOBBY
d. INASU
e. ROSILY
f. MANI
g. PUSHPAM

6. KUNJAMMA
W/O. DEVASSY KONIKKARA

7. KOCHUMARIYAM
W/O. OUSEPH KONIKKARA

8. KUNJANAM
W/O. VARGHESE CHITHALAN

9. KUNJILAKUTTY
W/O. PAPPU PUTHENANGADY

10. KUNJETHY
W/O. GEORGE MAMPULLY

11. ROSAKUTTY
W/O. CHAKORU PULIKKAN

12. ELYAKUTTY
W/O. KUNJUVAREED CHANDY

Compiled By : Joje Cherian Nadakavukaran

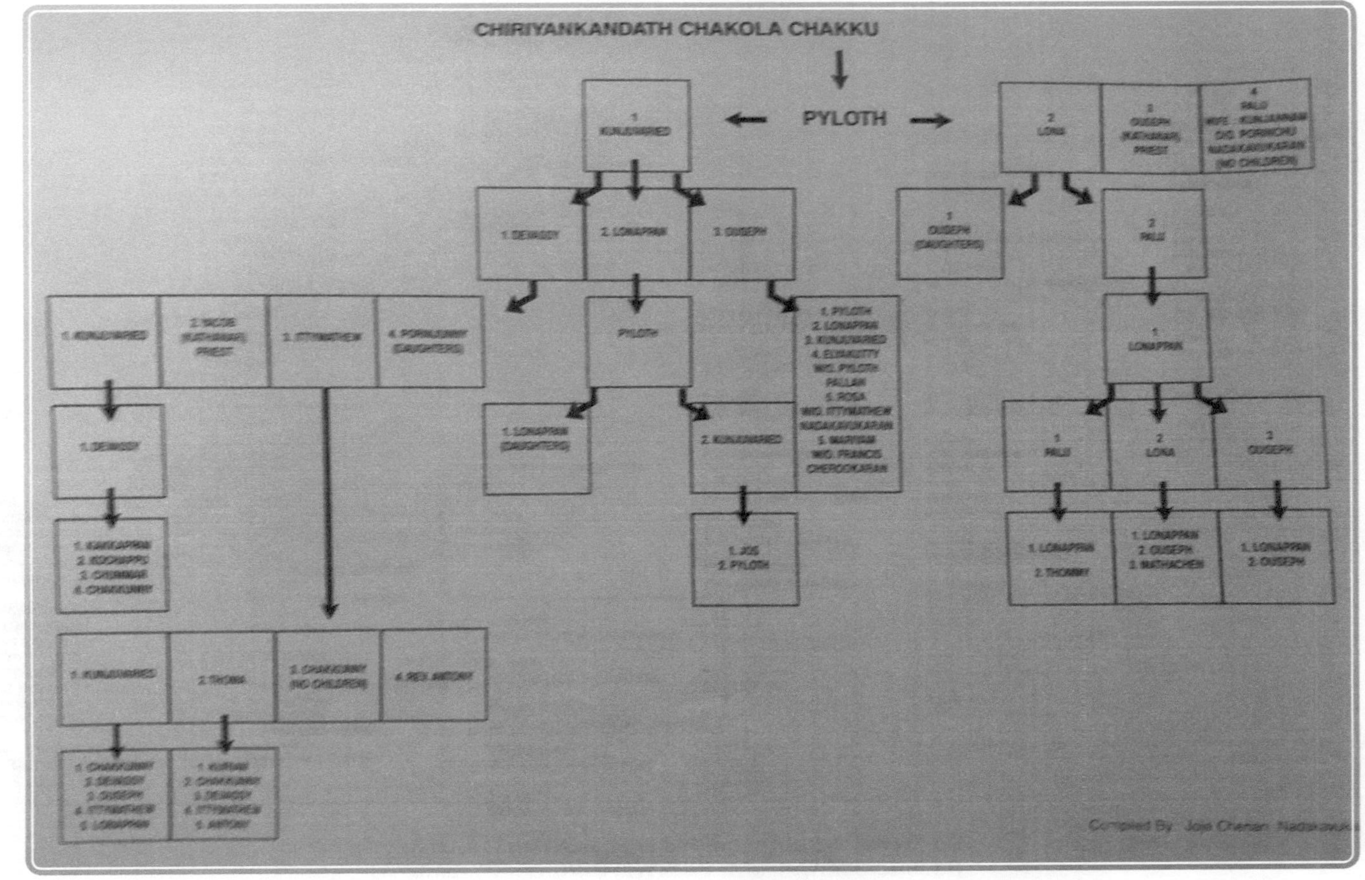

CHIRIYANKANDATH CHAKOLA CHAKKU

PYLOTH

1 KUNJUVARIED
2 LONA
3 OUSEPH (KATHANAR) PRIEST
4 PALU WIFE : KUNJUNNAN D/O PORINCHU NADAKAVUKARAN (NO CHILDREN)

1. DEVASSY
2. LONAPPAN
3. OUSEPH

1 OUSEPH (DAUGHTERS)
2 PALU

PYLOTH

1. PYLOTH
2. LONAPPAN
3. KUNJUVARIED
4. ELISAKUTTY W/O PYLOTH PALLAN
5. ROSA W/O ITTYMATHEW NADAKAVUKARAN
5. MARIAM W/O FRANCIS CHEROOKARAN

1 LONAPPAN (DAUGHTERS)
2. KUNJUVARIED

1. JOS
2. PYLOTH

1 LONAPPAN

1 PALU
2 LONA
3 OUSEPH

1. LONAPPAN
2. THOMMY

1. LONAPPAN
2. OUSEPH
3. MATHACHEN

1. LONAPPAN
2. OUSEPH

1. KUNJUVARIED
2. YACOB (KATHANAR) PRIEST
3. ITTYMATHEW
4. PORINCHY (DAUGHTERS)

1. DEVASSY

1. KANJAPPAN
2. KOCHAPPU
3. CHUMMAR
4. CHAKKUNNY

1. KUNJUVARIES
2. THOMA
3. CHAKKUNNY (NO CHILDREN)
4. REX ANTONY

1. CHAKKUNNY
2. DEVASSY
3. OUSEPH
4. ITTYMATHEW
5. LONAPPAN

1. KURIAN
2. CHAKKUNNY
3. DEVASSY
4. ITTYMATHEW
5. ANTONY

Compiled By: Jose Cheran Nadakavukaran

CHIRIYANKANDATH CHAKOLA KUNJUVARIED OUSEPH
WIFE : ELIAKUTTY, ALAPPAT PALATHINGAL, KATTOOR

PYLOTH
WIFE : ROSA KUTTIKADAN

1. KUNJILAKUTTY
a. ROSAKUTTY
W/O. LAZAR PAYYOOR :-
BABU PAUL
THAMPI FRANCIS
ROLLY VARGHESE
PATRICK ANIYAN
VINCENT UNNI

2. MARIYAM
W/O. PYLOTH CHIRAYATH :-
PAUL
THOMAS
LISSY MATHEW
IRINE MATHEW

LONAPPAN
WIFE : ITTIANAM
D/O. NADAKAVUKARAN INASU
VARUNNY

1. KOCHAPPU
a. JOHNY :-
BABY, PAUL, NEENA
b. JACOB
c. GEORGE :-
JOS, VIGI
d. SOSAMMA
W/O. FRANCIS THATTIL
(ANDREWS)
e. INASU :-
SUBIN, REBIN
f. PAUL :-
DEEPA, JACOB

2. INASU
a. KOCHUTTY
W/O. ERINJERY KURIAPPAN
b. LALAMMA
W/O. MANNUKADAN DAVY
c. SAMUEL :-
INASU, VARGHESE
d. SARAKUTTY
W/O. OLLUKARAN PAVOO
e. MAGGY
W/O. AKKARA KURIAPPAN
f. BABY
W/O. PULIKKOTTIL THOMAS
g. KESSY
W/O. PANAKKAL SAMSON
h. PREMY
W/O. CHAKOLA DAVIS

3. KOCHUPYLOTH
a. LEELA
W/O. JOY CHETTUPUZHAKKARAN
b. LONAPPAN :-
PAUL, PRIYA
c. VARGHESE :- PAUL
d. ANNIE
W/O. BOSCO ALAPPAT

KUNJUVAREED
WIFE : KUNJAMMA
D/O. IMMATTY ANTONY

1. OUSEPH
(NO CHILDREN)

2. PYLOTH
a. GEORGE
b. LEELA
W/O. GEORGE CHANDY
c. MEENA
W/O. JOSHY VERATTOLA

3. ANTHONYKUTTY
a. VARGHESE
b. MARIYAMA
W/O. JAISON CHIROTHA
c. ANITHA

4. KOCHELIAKUTTY
W/O. ANTONY VELLANIKKARAN

5. SARA
W/O. THOMAS MANNUKADAN

4. MARIYAM
W/O. LONAPPAN THALOKARAN

5. ACHAI
W/O. VAREED NALLENGARA

6. ELIAKUTTY
W/O. MELADATH POZHATH OUSEPH

7. ROSAKUTTY
W/O. JACOB CHERUKARAN

8. KUNJETHY
W/O. JACOB VENGASSERY

ELIAKUTTY
W/O. PYLOTH PALLAN

1. ANTONY
a. PAUL
b. KOCHAPPU
c. ANTO

2. JOSEPH
a. PAUL
b. FRANCIS
c. ANTONY

3. KUNJILAKUTTY
W/O. PYLOTH CHALISSERY

4. MARIYAM
W/O. KUNDUKULAM LONAPPAN

5. KUNJANAM
W/O. PERINJERY ANTHAPPAN

6. KUNJAMMA
W/O. PULLOKARAN THOMAS

7. ROSAKUTTY
W/O. THOTTUNGAL JOSEPH

8. ELIAKUTTY
W/O. ANTONY PULIKKAN

9. THRESSIAMMA
W/O. JOSEPH MECHERY

ROSA
W/O. ITTYMATHEW NADAKAVUKARAN

1. REV. N.I. JOSEPH
a. MATHEW
b. JOHN

2. MARIYAM
W/O. DEVASSY CHAMMANAM

3. KUNJETHY
W/O. REV. PAULOSE KONIKKARA

4. IGNATIUS
a. ITTYMATHEW
b. JOSE
c. JOHN
d. BOBBY

5. ELIAKUTTY
W/O. JOSEPH THATTIL

6. DAVID
a. ITTYMATHEW
b. MOHAN
c. ABI
d. ROSAKUTTY
e. RAJAMMA

7. SARA
W/O. GEORGE IMMATTY

8. GEORGE
a. MATHEW
b. INASU
c. JOSE

9. ROSAKUTTY
W/O. KURIAN CHANDY

10. JOHN

11. KURIAN
a. ITTYMATHEW
b. JOHN
c. JOJU

12. PAUL
a. SEBI
b. ABI
c. JOHN

13. CHERIAN
a. SHAJI
b. JOJE

14. FRANCIS
a. ITTYMATHEW
b. ANTONY
c. JOHN

MARIYAM
W/O. FRANCIS CHERUKARAN

1. KOCHAPPU
(NO CHILDREN)

2. LAZAR
a. JOY
b. JOICY
c. FRANCIS
d. MINI

3. THRESSIA
W/O. PAUL MOONJELY

4. ACHAI
W/O. JOSEPH PAYYAPPILLY

5. ROSY
W/O. PAUL PARAMBAN

6. INASU
a. MARTIN
b. BLESSY

Compiled By : Joje Cherian Nadakavukaran

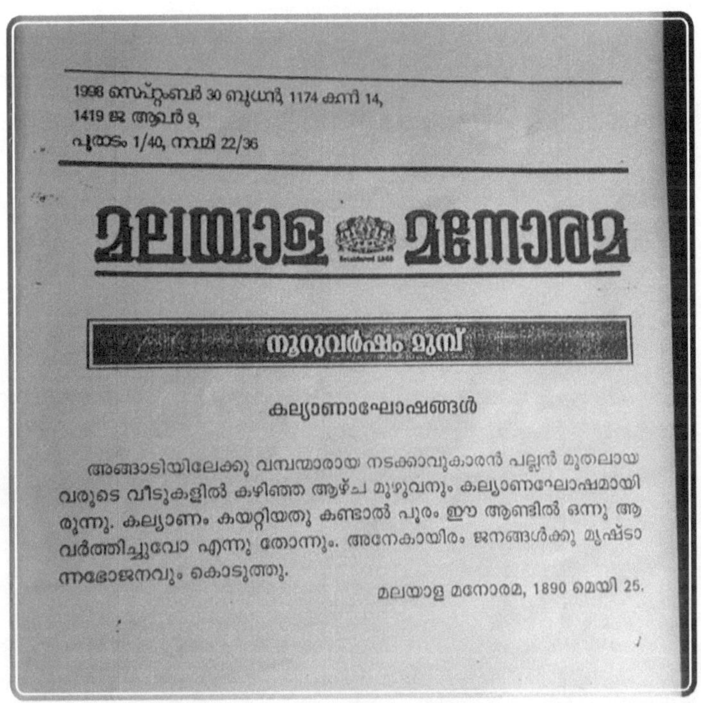

This is about an article came in Malayalam Manorama Newspaper, describing about a grand wedding celebration happened in our family in May25, 1890 attended by Thousands of guests. Comparing this event with famous festival "Trichur Pooram" in Kerala State.